The
SMALL
INVESTOR'S
Guide to
Making Money
in Canadian
Real Estate

The
SMALL
INVESTOR'S
Guide to
Making Money
in Canadian
Real Estate

Gary Weiss

Third Revised Edition

Third revised edition published in 1992 by
Stoddart Publishing Co. Limited
34 Lesmill Road
Toronto, Canada
M3B 2T6
(416) 445-3333

First published in 1987 by
Stoddart Publishing Co. Limited
First revised edition published 1988
Second revised edition published 1989

Canadian Cataloguing in Publication Data
Weiss, Gary
   The small investor's guide to making money in Canadian real
estate

3rd rev. ed.
ISBN 0-7737-5553-5

1. Real estate investment—Canada. I. Title.

HD316.W44 1992   332.63'24'0971   C92-095429-4

Cover Design: Graphisphere Inc.
Typesetting: Jay Tee Graphics Ltd.

Printed in Canada

Stoddart Publishing gratefully acknowledges the support of
the Canada Council, Ontario Ministry of Culture and
Communications, Ontario Arts Council and Ontario Publishing
Centre in the development of writing and publishing in Canada.

Contents

Preface
to the Third Revised Edition

Whew! What a ride Canadian real estate has experienced since this book was first published in 1987. Like a rodeo bareback rider in very slow motion, prices and activity soared for two years, then abruptly plunged as the bronco kicked. Lots of small investors — and some very big ones — got bucked off.

We're now, say the pundits of yesterday's editorial pages, supposedly in a new era of low inflation and deflated ambition. And so real estate is a washed-up investment relic. Time to junk your aspirations and wrap yourself in a veil of gloom?

Certainly not.

To begin with, the recent recession's effects on real estate have not been uniform — either by category or geography. True, office space in downtown Montreal goes begging. In Toronto, one owner apparently even walked away from a 20-story tower. Yes, residential vacancies rose. But plunging mortgage rates gave landlords the opportunity to finance at rates that make even much lower rents profitable. And at the same time that southern Ontario home prices dropped 25% from their peak, prices in B.C.'s lower mainland rebounded quite nicely in 1991 and 1992.

Second, the economic misfortune wrought on some has been equally opportune for others. The truth is that many of the houses and, particularly, condominiums that went the power of sale/foreclosure route were owned by short-term speculators who took their chances. Don't discount rolling the dice for a short-term gain. But in real estate, there's no substitute for taking the long view with conservative assumptions.

And the long-term view is that, whether in one nation or two, the 26.7 million residents north of the 49th parallel will continue to generate a tremendous need for space in which to live, work and play.

Preface
to the First Edition

The Small Investor's Guide to Making Money in Canadian Real Estate is designed to give the individual investor a hands-on guide to the exciting world of Canadian real estate investment. It examines the rewards — and pitfalls — of directly investing in various kinds of real estate: houses and everything from condominiums to strip plazas and apartment buildings.

It is written with the individual investor in mind — the person who, in real estate, is called the "small" investor. In real estate "small" means something quite different than in the rest of the world. A stake of $500,000 cash will impress your stockbroker, but in our major cities, you're still a "small" real estate investor.

"What can you get for $1 million?" muses a commercial real estate broker. "Three or four stores. Nothing much, really."

You may need a multi-million dollar nest egg to impress him. But if your aim is more modest — say, adding $20,000, $50,000 or $100,000 extra to your annual income, you can do very well indeed.

I am convinced that the careful individual investor can make more money with less risk through direct property investment than through any other (supposedly) comparable investment. This book is designed to show you in plain English some of the specific ways and means of doing so.

* * *

By its nature, the acquisition, management, development and disposition of real property is intricately bound up in tax and real estate law. While this book touches on a number of these areas, it is emphasized here that these references are for general information only. Tax and real estate law and policies are constantly changing. As importantly, each transaction and each individual's tax situation is different. So before making any decisions, you should consult with your own trusted tax and/or legal advisor.

This edition contains revisions in accord with the February 1992 federal budget statement.

CHAPTER 1

Why Real Estate Is a Good Investment

"So my home has gone up in price. How does that help me? If I sell, I'll just have to pay more for a new one."

———

"Now is not the time to buy real estate. Prices are not going anywhere. They haven't for years. It's better to wait."

———

"Buy real estate now? Are you kidding? Prices are going up every day. It's all artificial. It's bound to collapse. It just *has* to."

———

Do these sentiments sound familiar? Of course; you've heard them before —

- notwithstanding that some of the greatest North American fortunes have been built on real estate;
- notwithstanding that properly selected real estate is one of the safest investments you can make;
- notwithstanding that real estate is just about the last tax haven available to the average-income person;
- and notwithstanding that real estate is valued so highly that it is the biggest single investment most Canadian families own.

Inertia — the tendency to remain in the same state without change — is the most comfortable condition for most of us. Excuses for not changing anything are as trite as they are familiar.

But hesitancy about investing in real estate is almost inconceivable when you consider the extent to which Canadians are already real estate investors without often realizing it. In 1991, 62.6% of private

1

Canadian households (accounting for 70% of all people) lived in their own homes, a figure exceeded only in the United States.[1] Total personal real estate investment — everything from condominiums to family farms and vacation cottages — is more than $150 billion.

Over the years the investment in personal shelter has paid off handsomely. For many retired Canadians, a paid-off home is the one thing that has made retirement on meagre pension plans affordable. For most people, their own home is their single biggest investment. And frequently a profitable one.

The average Canadian resale home price for 1975 was a mere $32,328. By 1985, the average had jumped 144.4% to $79,000 and by July 1992, the average had soared nearly 90%, to $149,525.[2] By contrast, during the same period the Consumer Price Index rose 117.5%.[3] In some cities, the gains in housing prices were double that. And, narrowing the focus, specific neighborhoods and sub-neighborhoods have shown even more spectacular gains.

For example, the mean average price for a central Toronto home in 1966 was $24,133; by 1975, it had risen to $64,325; and by July 1989, it had soared 465%, to $363,262. During the recent recession, the 1991 average dropped to $316,062, still giving a 391% increase over 1975.[4]

Over a five- to ten-year period, carefully selected, conventionally financed residential real estate in large cities has shown a far greater gain than comparable fixed investments. If, for instance, you bought the "average" Vancouver home in April 1975 for $57,763, by April 1985 it would have been worth $121,089.[5] To be conservative, you could have bought the house with a 25% down payment — $14,440. That would have given you a gross gain of $106,649.

If you had instead put your down payment into a one-year guaranteed investment certificate (GIC) and rolled-over the capital and interest each year, it would have grown to approximately $39,804.[6]

Even this comparison omits the net rental income and tax benefits the property would have yielded. Furthermore, by borrowing more than 25% of the purchase price, your return on money invested could have been even higher.

To be fair, your net gain on the property will have been lowered by interest costs on the mortgage, "transaction costs" — the real estate commission on sale, legal fees and transfer taxes, as well as the cost of maintenance over the period you owned it.[7]

Helen, a Toronto investor, could tell you about real estate versus the stock market. In the early 1980s she made $85,000 in Western Canadian oil stocks, then lost it all plus $24,000 of her original investment in the crash of world oil prices. During the same period, she bought three single-family downtown Toronto homes for a total of $179,000. She used $30,000 of her own money and borrowed the rest;

and she has since spent about $20,000 in renovations. The homes are now worth a total of $650,000. So their overall value has nearly quadrupled — and her original investment in them has risen thirteen-fold. Meanwhile, the properties have returned her more than $10,000 a year in net rental income. Commercial real estate, too, has racked up good gains over the past decade. For example, office rental rates for high-quality buildings in major markets have doubled and tripled, before falling back 30% through 1990-91.[8]

Investors who held on to land capable of being developed for industrial and commercial uses have prospered too. In 1976, for example, industrial land in Metropolitan Toronto ranged from approximately $85,000-$110,000 per acre. By 1986, it had risen to $150,000-$300,000 an acre and by 1989 the figures soared to $450,000-$750,000, before falling back 30% in 1990-91.[9]

Real estate's attractiveness as an investment is a combination of four major factors:

1. Cash Flow

In contrast to other common investments, real estate offers you the possibility of earning substantial periodic payments of cash over the life of the investment — not just a capital gain when you dispose of it.

While the dividend yield of the TSE composite was in the low 3% range in 1992, even investors in premium multi-family buildings currently expect at least 5% to 6% back yearly on their invested capital.

Although cash flow is derived from the rental income the property generates, it is *not* the same as the net rental income (gross rents minus carrying costs and taxes). Cash flow is not just a fancy way of saying income: it refers to the actual cash you receive in your hands over the life of the investment. You can have very little income, but a substantial cash flow mainly as a result of the tax advantages of owning real estate.

2. Tax Advantages

The tax advantages of owning real estate, whether it's for personal or investment use, take several forms:

1. Low taxation rates on capital gains — If you're not a professional investor — in other words, if real estate investment is not your main source of income or principal activity — usually not all your capital gains are taxed. Instead, 75% of your gains are counted as income subject to taxation. (As explained below, however, any individual real estate transaction may attract full taxes if it's deemed to be in the nature of a business.)

2. Lifetime capital gains exemption — The centrepiece of the Conservative government's 1985 budget was a phased-in $500,000

4

"lifetime" capital gains exemption. The exemption was immediately barraged by Liberal and New Democratic critics as a "giveaway" to the rich. Eventually, in the 1987 tax reform, a lifetime turned out to be three years, as the Conservatives "capped" the tax exemption at the 1987 limit of $100,000.[10]

And, in 1992, the Conservatives went further, abolishing the exemption for real estate altogether. According to budget papers, the goal of disqualifying real estate was to "help direct resources into productive investments which enhance Canada's ability to compete in international markets."

However, capital gains on real estate you bought before the end of February 1992 are still partially exempt. When you sell, your taxable gains are pro-rated on the ratio of the number of months you owned the property before March 1, 1992, to the total number of months you owned the property. For example, say you bought a property in March 1982 and sell it in March 1993 for a net capital gain of $100,000. The ratio is 120/132.

A	Capital Gain	$100,000
B	Number of months held before March 1992	120
	Total number of months held	132
Tax exempt gain A × B =		$90,909
Taxable Gain		$9,091
Taxable Amount (75%)		$6,818
Tax at a 49% combined bracket		$3,341

If you hold the property for just another year before taking the same capital gain, the ratio becomes 120/144.

A	Capital Gain	$100,000
B	Number of months held before March 1992	120
	Total number of months held	144
Tax exempt gain A × B =		$83,333
Taxable Gain		$16,667
Taxable Amount (75%)		$12,500
Tax at a 49% combined bracket		$6,125

In a stagnant market, the extra taxes quickly eat into any gains.
As the tables illustrate, the longer you own a property, the more

tax it will attract — even if it never appreciates in value after the 1992 cut-off date. Thus, as long as you can benefit from the capital gains lifetime exemption, if you have a property with little potential for gain, you have incentive to sell it sooner than later. Likewise, if you are planning to leave taxable property to heirs, you may wish to arrange for a transfer to them or to a holding company now. Otherwise, a later transfer will mean paying higher taxes.

Income you get from real estate trusts, corporations and real estate mutual funds that distribute capital gains dividends is also caught by the tax change.

You can only claim capital gains exemption to the extent that the gain exceeds your net cumulative investment losses after 1987.[11] This means that at the end of the year, all your investment expenses are subtracted from all your investment income. If this results in a loss, you have to deduct it from any capital gains that would have been eligible for exemption that year or in the future. Investment expenses consist of deductions for: interest; losses arising from renting or leasing property; your share of deductions attributable to passive participation in flow-through shares or Canadian exploration or resource expenses; carrying charges in passive co-ownership or limited partnership arrangements. Investment income consists of: interest, taxable dividends and property income; your share of passive limited partnership and other co-ownership income; income from renting or leasing of real estate.

Tax exempt capital gains up to $500,000 are still permitted from the sale of a family farm, provided you, your spouse or children used the land for farming for five years after 1972.

The 1987 tax reform also increased the cumulative share exemption for shares of small business corporations (essentially Canadian-controlled private corporations active in Canada) to $500,000 at the beginning of 1988. To qualify for the exemption, the shares can't be held outside your own family for the 24 months prior to sale. For the real estate minded, this exemption may encourage business people to buy their own premises; and for real estate investors, an incentive to get involved in other businesses as well.

What if, as a result of taxable capital gains, your net income in one year is a lot more than you expect to be reporting in future years? Prior to the 1987 tax reform, you could "forward average" income to future years, when you might be in a lower tax bracket. But, in the interest of " simplification," the 1987 reform abolished forward averaging after the 1987 tax year. So be sure to take this into account when selling property that might result in taxable capital gains. You might, for instance, end up with more after tax dollars, by delaying a sale to the following year.

Any capital gains you make as a result of real estate transactions that are *in the nature of a business*, as defined in the *Income Tax Act*, are still taxed as regular income. Even if you are not a professional real estate trader, an isolated transaction may still be taxed as business income. A gain on the sale of undeveloped land is almost always likely to attract full taxation. In any case, according to Revenue Canada the courts have used the following criteria in figuring whether a profit is income or capital:

Period of ownership — Property held for a short time will be deemed to have been purchased for the purposes of resale while property held for a long time is more likely to be considered an investment.

Frequency of similar transactions — An extensive history of buying and selling similar properties is evidence that you're a trader in real estate.

Improvement and development work — Laying sewers, building roads or preparing a plan of subdivision indicates a business venture.

Reason for the sale — Actively marketing the property indicates a business. But if you sell as the result of something unexpected (e.g., sudden need of money or expropriation) the profit may still be considered a capital gain.

Relation to your ordinary business — Real estate agents and builders have a harder time proving profit is capital rather than income.[12]

None of the points above are conclusive in themselves, but are considered in relation to all the facts of each case. The overriding test is your *intention* when you bought the property. Intention is something that Revenue Canada or the courts determine in each case.

For example, say you bought an apartment building in order to earn rental income. But it didn't work out, so you sold it for a nice profit. Is your profit taxable as income or capital? You might claim you had no choice but to sell it as it was losing money, so your profit is capital gain. But if it's determined that you had the *secondary* intention to sell it for profit in case you couldn't make money on the rental, the profits will usually be taxed as business income, says Revenue Canada.

3. *Depreciation* — Along with the benefit on capital gains, property owners can utilize *capital cost allowance* (depreciation).

You can deduct a fixed percentage of the acquisition cost and capital additions to real estate as an expense against the property. The idea is to reflect the property's declining value as a result of wear, deterioration and obsolescence. But as depreciation is a *non-cash expense*, the capital cost allowance effectively increases your cash flow. Three further points to keep in mind: (i) You cannot use depreciation to create or increase a rental loss; (ii) You cannot depreciate land, only the buildings and other improvements on it. Brick buildings can be depreciated at 4% a year,[13] wood structures acquired before 1979 — or after 1979 if without footings or foundations — at 10% a year; (iii) if you sell the property for more than its depreciated value, whatever capital cost allowance you have taken is *recaptured*.[14] But until that day, you can put that additional cash flow to work making you more money. Or just buy yourself a pink Cadillac.

4. Business expense deductions — As a landlord, you can deduct *current* expenses from rental income in the year you pay them. Deductible expenses include:

- property taxes
- insurance premiums
- heat, light and water bills
- salaries and wages to superintendents etc.
- accounting services
- legal fees (but not those connected with buying the property)
- commissions to rental and collection agents
- landscaping costs
- payments to tenants to cancel their leases
- interest on money borrowed to buy or improve the property[15]
- certain auto expenses
- maintenance and repairs (but not the value of your own labor).

The last two deductions are particularly advantageous to the small investor. You probably own a car or truck anyway. But by using the vehicle(s) in your property business, you'll be able to legitimately deduct many of your ownership costs. However if you only have one rental property and it's in the general area where you live, you'll have to personally do all or part of the repairs and maintenance to get the deduction. Simply collecting rents doesn't count. But if you own two or more rental properties, you can deduct expenses for the purpose of collecting rents and generally providing management.

Any money you spend for maintenance and repairs is deductible from income as long as it's a *current expense*, not a *capital expense*.

Capital expenses are added to the building's undepreciated capital cost and can only be deducted within the allowable limits. Anything that improves or enhances the original value or usefulness of a building is usually treated as a capital expense. By contrast, repairs take place after a breakdown and maintenance is the general upkeep of an asset.

Your special tax advantage as an investor in real estate?

It's clear that repairs and maintenance can increase the market value and cash flow of a property while being fully deductible in the year you pay for them. To illustrate: painting and patching walls, sanding floors, fixing leaky plumbing and just doing a thorough cleaning can add thousands of dollars to the resale value of a property, or the rent you can get for it. So, in effect, you can get the benefits of a capital addition without the drawback of only being able to deduct it over many years.

But keep in mind two points: (a) money you spend to put a newly acquired older building into rentable condition is regarded as a capital expense; (b) repairs you make in anticipation of selling property or that are a condition of the sale are regarded as capital expenses *unless* the repairs would have been made in any event.[16]

5. Real estate losses deductible against other income. Ordinarily, you can reduce your other taxable income by losses you incur in your real estate investments. As explained in point 4 above, although the immediate loss is real, the eventual effect may be positive. Meanwhile, you pay lower taxes.

6. Tax exemption of imputed income on your principal residence — Imputed income is the untaxed benefit owners of capital goods derive from their ownership. Applied to homes, it means the net benefit that you derive from owning your own home — in other words, the rent you would have to pay for your home if you didn't own it, minus maintenance, taxes, mortgage interest etc.

The reasoning is that if, for instance, your employer provided you with housing, you would expect to count it as income and be taxed accordingly. But as a homeowner, you "receive" the self-same benefits free of tax.

Although many housing experts object to the whole idea, net imputed income has been recognized as a tax omission by many economists. In fact, imputed rental income is taxed in some European countries. After looking at how this exemption works, economist George Fallis concludes that the "typical taxpayer has a clear incentive to own rather than rent housing and to place all savings in housing equity rather than bonds."[17]

7. Principal residence capital gains tax exemption — Lastly, your own home is your surest and most lucrative real estate tax benefit. Any capital gain you make from selling your principal residence, including one-half hectare (1.2355 acres) of surrounding property, is usually non-taxable, though you must report it. You are limited to one tax-free sale of a principal residence per calendar year.[18]

Besides eliminating taxes, the capital gains exemption "intensifies the bidding (and price increases) in the housing market," points out urban land economist David Baxter.[19] This incentive of tax-free gains combined with the intense attachment to home ownership are key reasons why single-family housing remains a very attractive investment for the smaller property investor. By contrast, in the former Iron Curtain countries, housing was an item of consumption allocated by the state in accordance with the individual's "needs."

3. Appreciation

Appreciation is simply the tendency of real estate to grow in value over the years. But because real estate is "non-fungible" — that is, it's not interchangeable like bushels of wheat — it's impossible to devise a meaningful average of price increases that will have anything more than a general application to a specific piece of property.

Similarly, it's probably impossible to accurately compare returns on real estate investment with returns on other types of investment. A number of studies have attempted to do this employing selected samples of institutional investments. But a leading analyst who has picked apart these studies could only conclude that over time, "the returns from real estate as a class of investments should correspond closely to the returns from common stock investment."[20]

And as with securities investments, in the short-term, real estate values can fall and even evaporate entirely.

4. Leverage

This is a fancy way of saying that a small amount of money can give you control over a relatively large asset. You can typically leverage from 75% to 90% — that is, borrow from 75% to 90% of the purchase price in the form of a mortgage loan(s). In contrast to the stock market, if the value of the property falls, the lender usually has no recourse to you — unless, of course, you don't continue making your mortgage payments.

Leverage also *magnifies the return you* can get on your money. Say you buy a house and in the first year it rises 6% in value. If you bought it for all cash, you've only increased the value of your investment by 6%. But if you bought it utilizing high-ratio financing, your return could be as much as 120%. You measure your gain or loss against the actual amount you've put in, not the total cost of the investment. Consider the following table:

TABLE I

Effects of Leverage

Assume you buy a $100,000 home and that it increases in value 6% a year. Here's what your return on your initial cash investment would be, expressed as a percentage, depending on the percentage of the purchase price you borrowed.

Return on Initial Cash (expressed as a %) of

Value of Property after		Amount Borrowed			
		Nil	50%	75%	90%
One year	$106,000	6%	12%	24%	60%
Five years	$133,820	30%	68%	135%	338%
Ten years	$179,080	79%	158%	316%	791%

To take advantage of this leverage, you don't have to have a high-income or assets — just credit enough to borrow and the ability to correctly evaluate risks.

Economist Baxter singles out another advantage of real estate investment: "Monopolistic or oligopolistic powers do not exist within real property markets."[21] Property ownership — and especially home ownership — is widely distributed. So is the demand for ownership. And while much has been made of the concentration of developable land, and the supposed monopoly profits it entails, new housing accounts for less than 3% of the total supply.

In other words, when it comes to real estate, the small investor is on an even footing with the larger investor. That's something that no one would dream of saying with relation to the stock market.

But will prices continue to rise now that inflation is down to 1½-2% a year? Is real estate wealth based on capital appreciation a vanishing dream?

Not likely. Not as long as investors are allowed to use and profit from the continuing availability of leverage; special opportunities that are common to real estate because of its highly open nature; the moneymaking power of creativity in negotiating and financing the purchase and sale of real estate; and in adapting real estate from less efficient to more efficient uses.

By using leverage, even small gains in the overall price of the property can become big returns on the money you have invested. Say you buy a $100,000 home with $25,000 down and hold it for five years during which the annual inflation rate is only 4%. By the end of the fifth year, the price of the house would have risen to $121,665. But if you've put down just 25%, you've almost doubled your money in five years. If you've put down 15% ($15,000), you've increased your investment 144%.

Even if inflation were to continue at 2%, leverage would still work its wonders. Here are the effects of leverage assuming a 2% annual inflation rate and a $100,000 property.

TABLE 2

Value of Property after		Nil	Gain on Equity (expressed as a % of amount borrowed) 50%	75%	90%
One year	$102,000	2	4	8	20
Five years	$110,408	10.4	20.8	41.6	104.1
Ten years	$121,899	21.9	43.8	87.6	219

Although it's useful to know what average rates of inflation are, it's just as important to know that they are just that — average. The "open" nature of the real estate market continuously provides opportunities that negate the averages.

In contrast to investing in, say the commodity market, each property has unique characteristics that immediately affect its economic value, which are:

1. *Location* — This includes the relationship of any improvements (buildings, landscaping etc.) to the site; and the relationship of the site to the community it's in.

2. *Physical characteristics of the improvements* — Even new homes in a peapod subdivision are quickly differentiated. Landscaping, decoration, additions and even housekeeping alter their relative values.

3. *Economic structure of the investment* — This includes the nature of any debt obligations. Are there mortgages? What rates of interest do they carry? What are their terms? Are there tenants or not? What are the terms of their leases? How reliable are the tenants?

4. *Management ability of the property owner* — Some investors couldn't manage a doghouse without losing money; others can create profit where none existed before and convert meagre returns into rich rivers of cash.

Economically speaking, real estate investment markets are inefficient; information is not instantly and uniformly available to every investor. So the well-informed investor who moves decisively and knowledgeably always stands to profit first from new opportunities.

Average Home Prices (in $000)

	1975	1980	1984	1987*	1989	1992**
Victoria	N.A.	85.34	90.85	103.80	142.91	197.52
Vancouver	57.76	100.07	113.72	136.60	209.67	248.01
Calgary	48.34	93.98	86.72	95.10	112.84	126.46
Edmonton	43.85	84.64	79.15	76.19	89.05	112.13
Regina	33.88	48.63	58.89	67.15	72.08	70.67
Saskatoon	N.A.	60.50	67.08	71.52	75.70	74.34
Winnipeg	33.46	51.06	59.11	80.36	84.23	81.82
Toronto	57.58	75.62	102.35	193.81	273.70	209.30
Hamilton	N.A.	58.09	65.91	117.20	163.25	147.56
Ottawa	49.66	63.18	102.08	115.57	137.46	146.97
Montreal	35.27	49.42	64.44	97.46	110.02	115.59
Halifax	N.A.	57.84	78.47	87.23	93.44	101.29
St. John's	N.A.	53.25	61.54	75.78	83.57	94.36

* December price

** August prices.   Source: Canadian Real Estate Association

CHAPTER 2

What You Need to Succeed in Real Estate

You've probably heard of this person. Everyone has. He's the one who bought that patch of farmland that seven years later became a regional shopping center. Or she picked up half a dozen homes in a rundown area two years ago, then miraculously the neighborhood became a hotbed of renovators, and she's made a fortune. Or perhaps he bought a decrepit downtown warehouse, then renovated it into a successful restaurant, or even a budding international chain.

Some guys have all the luck!

If only you had seen the opportunities, you too could be reaping the reward. So why is it that some people always seem to be in the right place at the right time. Is it a natural skill? Or can you too learn to spot good real estate investment opportunities?

Real estate analyst and money manager Ira Gluskin of Gluskin, Sheff & Associates, replies, only somewhat tongue in cheek, "It's like saying, 'How can you learn to be tall?' You have to be basically smart. For example, everybody wants to be downtown today. But that's been a trend for at least ten years. The people who recognized it first are the ones who really cashed in."

Perhaps there's some gimmick, many people think. There isn't. But there are certain characteristics that mark the successful investor; certain attitudes and ways of looking at market facts. And there are some specific things that the successful investor looks for in locating the profitable investment.

Assuming you're basically smart, what then? You need four things: (1) money; (2) connections; (3) time; (4) a propensity for risk taking.

1. Money isn't the obstacle many people think it is. There's no reason your first investments have to be large. The remarkable advantage of real estate is that it is a leveraged investment. You use other people's money to make you money. And while leverage can sink

13

you, you'll usually stand to lose no more than you put in. *Provided you're in for the long haul.* Speculative investments that can make you rich can just as easily make you poor. Investors in southern Ontario commercial real estate in the 1988–89 boom — even those with as much as 50% equity — saw their investments jeopardized as interest rates rose and vacancies abounded. Purely speculative house "flippers" were trapped as house prices plummeted up to 50%.

2. Connections. Good ones count. But you don't have to be born with them. You can create them. Speaking with knowledgeable real estate brokers and agents will clue you in to what's happening. Look at what's available and what properties are selling for. Similarly, if you're looking for, say, commercial properties, besides dealing with agents you can contact local business people in the area you're interested in.

3. Time is another essential ingredient. You have to be willing to spend it learning the market: looking at areas for general impressions. Looking at specific properties for possible purchase. Looking through new listings for price comparisons. It means driving the streets, walking the commercial blocks, going into shopping centers, office buildings, strip plazas. You can't invest in property from your home computer terminal. Professional investors spend a lot of their time on the move, simply nosing out deals and inspecting properties. That's the only way to learn the market and there's no substitute for thorough market knowledge. That way, when the right deal does come up, you can act on it immediately with confidence.

Along those lines, Alana, an investor in single family homes, got a call from an agent late one night about a new office listing that he thought she might be interested in. The agent picked her up at midnight, dusty from the renovation she was working on. The next morning she put in an offer and got the property for perhaps 10% to 12% less than it would have gone for had there been other bidders on the home. She put down $10,000 on the $70,000 house; rents carried the expenses on the property. Three years later, her $70,000 income-earning investment was worth about $150,000 — thus multiplying her initial investment eight-fold, even after taking into account such costs as legal fees, real estate commissions and transfer taxes.

If you're wedded to a nine-to-five job, you may face problems in finding the time to act quickly. But there's no reason why real estate investment shouldn't be a family affair and every reason why it should. One spouse may be good at scouting out locations and doing or directing renovation work, the other excellent at tenant relations.

4. A propensity for risk-taking. The ultimate ingredient is a turn of mind that isn't deterred by risk. Direct real estate investment is not a sure thing. And if you won't or can't move until you are sure you've covered every angle, every contingency, real estate investment just isn't for you. Every city is full of self-styled real estate "investors" who never actually buy anything. They've got the money, the connections, the time and the knowledge. But they don't have the courage. They just look and look and look. They phone for information on every ad and every sign they see. They know every street, every house and every real estate agent who'll listen to them. They also know every objection to every opportunity; and they never fail to heed the siren call to inaction.

"It's inconceivable to me that people could not have heard about the fortunes being made in real estate for decades, " says Gluskin. "Clearly they have avoided it because of the risks and time constraints in their own lives. The reason people don't open up the paper and take advantage of numerous opportunities is that they're not temperamentally disposed to do so."

Let's assume now that you've met the four basic criteria. What then?

Again, there's no magic. Essentially you're trying to look into the future configuration of the market. You're trying to divine what future demand will be for the property you will be buying now and selling later. Will home buyers want the type of home you're looking at? And will they be willing to pay more for it than you did? Will tenants want to rent your apartments? industrialists your factory or warehouse? retailers your stores? In other words, look at every property you're interested in with an eye to future demand.

Keys to spotting future high-demand areas include the following:

a) Industrial activity — Where industry goes, every other amenity follows. That means stores, offices, recreational facilities. A major new tourist attraction can have the same effect.

b) Major highway or rapid transit extension can also signal future development. Commuting time is cut down. Distant communities become accessible. A reverse situation could arise in a bedroom community. To ease local tax burdens, the community may decide to industrialize. Government incentives for industrial park development can also attract new industry.

c) A neighborhood changing for the better is a sure sign of investment possibilities. Downtown areas close to public transit and shopping are good bets. However, there may be more profit potential on the fringes of improving areas, before prices have pushed upward, than in an already established area. If you're looking at an upgraded area, look at all forms of real estate. Many investors, for instance, concentrate on home renovations while forgetting the nearby commercial strips that may in fact be better long-term investments.

d) *Large new shopping centers* — Many retailers like to go into these centers, but few are chosen. Either they can't afford the rents or they don't fit the center's "mix." If you can provide those retailers with nearby space, you'll both benefit from the draw of the larger center.

e) *Major resource developments* can boost real estate values. But boom town profits are precarious. Remember, too, when you're looking at remote locations, that the local wheeler-dealers have a headstart on the best deals at the best prices.

So, when you're weighing investments, don't get carried away with unusual or distant investments. When the larger developers were small, they used to say they wouldn't go anywhere they couldn't drive to in an hour. Now they're international, but their original idea still applies to the small investor.

Smart investing requires, to use popular economic terminology, taking both a micro and macro approach. On one hand, you should have an understanding of the major social, economic and political factors affecting real estate values. And on the other, you have to be able to assess the smallest details of the way a specific building is laid out and built.

You may be able to exactly forecast the path future development will take in your community. But if you can't distinguish between the wrong side of the tracks and the right, a house with bankable charm and one without, you'll forever be out of luck. And out of money.

CHAPTER 3

How to Measure Return When You Buy Property

No matter what kind of investment you make, you always want to earn a good return on it. Of course, just what is "good" depends on your expectations and on the nature of your investment.

With some investments, the return you get is fixed and easily established. If, for example, you put money into a government or corporate bond or into a guaranteed investment certificate or a mortgage, you know in advance what return you will get. Even if general interest levels fluctuate, at least you know what return you are earning at any given time.

But when it comes to real estate, "return" loses much of its certainty. You don't know what the rate of return will be. Partly, that's the nature of real estate. Each real estate investment is like a separate business and returns on each business are what you make them; you're not chained to a set figure. More than likely though, you may not know yourself exactly what you mean by return.

And this lack of knowledge can hurt you. For instance, newspaper advertisements for investment properties often quote return figures that sound attractive.

But do they refer to the return on cash actually invested? Before or after taxes? Before or after servicing any mortgages? They rarely specify exactly what they're referring to. One leading consultant gives 16 different definitions of real estate return. And even that's not an exhaustive list, he says.

However, the most common measure of return is variously known by three names — *Broker's equity return; cash on cash return; or return on investment*. What they all mean is simply the cash that you, the investor, get back each year on your initial investment — *after* debt servicing and operating expenses, but *before* paying income taxes.

Since it's a widely used measure of profitability, it's a useful starting point for comparing investments. For one thing, it's easy to figure

17

out. If you invest $100,000 and you get $9,000 back after paying your mortgages and expenses, you're getting a 9% cash on cash return. But even this straightforward definition poses problems.

For example, in calculating potential return on this basis, you could justifiably count such costs as prepaid interest, legal fees, brokerage costs and land transfer taxes as part of your initial investment. Indeed, these *are* capital expenses as far as Revenue Canada is concerned. But real estate agents and sellers of property almost always exclude these transaction costs from their calculations.

Other commonly used measures of return are: 1) *Free and clear return:* the net operating income divided by the purchase price — but *before* debt service and taxes; 2) *Payback period:* the time required to recover your initial investment. The shorter the payback period, the shorter the time your funds are at risk.

The problem with this method is that it says nothing about whether you'll ever get anything back beyond your original investment. Also, it downplays an investment with a long payback period that may, in the long run, outperform a project with a short payback period.

In any case, none of these commonly used measures takes into account other vital non-cash components of return you should be looking at, including:

Tax effects — Taxes of every sort are the largest single expenditure for most Canadians. So, not surprisingly, taxes affect real estate investment in just as big a way. To properly evaluate a real estate venture, you must consider all the tax effects of buying, holding and selling investment real estate.

Equity buildup, or amortization. This is the amount that you pay off on your mortgage financing over the period of your investment. Keep in mind, though, that this equity buildup is a *conditional* or deferred return. You only realize it when you sell or refinance the property. And then only if its market value has increased. If the property has dropped in value when you sell it, the money you've put in won't be recaptured.

Appreciation — an increase in the value of your property over time. Again, there's no guarantee you'll be able to sell the property for more than you paid for it. Appreciation is only a potential return.

Just how much can these indirect returns affect your calculations on profitability? Here's one illustration:

Assume a $20,000 equity investment in a $100,000 property, with the balance financed at 10% interest and amortized for 25 years; the property has a net income of $1,000 for the year and appreciates 5% a year. The tax benefit comes as a result of being able to reduce net income by taking capital cost allowance; the owner is in the 50% tax bracket. The following table shows various calculations of return after one year.

TABLE 4

(1) Net income	$1,000	5%
(2) Net income + tax effect	$1,000 $1,250	
	$2,250	11.25%
(3) Net income + tax effect + equity buildup	$1,000 $1,250 $ 800	
	$3,050	15.25%
(4) Net income + tax effect + equity buildup + appreciation	$1,000 $1,250 $ 800 $5,000	
	$8,100	40.5%

An even bigger jump in return would appear if, on sale, the capital gains were partially exempted from tax under the $100,000 capital gains exemption. MURB units might show even more tax benefits.

By all means, calculate all these variables. Only keep in mind that appreciation and equity buildup are always *conditional*.

Cash-on-cash figures presented in "brokers' setups" can also be as conditional as appreciation. A frequent problem is that they don't set enough aside for professional management. For instance, experienced investors and developers may need only 1.5% to 2% of gross income for management. But if you have to hire a professional management company, expect to pay 3% to 5% in fees for an apartment building, 10% for a house.

If you do the management yourself — and this is a good idea with small properties — you can save management fees. Just remember that this distorts the picture of the return on the property. You may be getting more money back, but part of it will be from your service as a manager, not as a return on your capital investment.

Vendors are likely also to minimize maintenance costs. For an apartment building, these costs will generally be in the range of 45% of rentals; the Ontario Residential Tenancy Commission has used ratios of up to 60%.

In going over the setup, check that it includes adequate reserves for replacement and repair. They may be non-cash costs for now. But don't delude yourself as to the property's real return by omitting them from your calculations.

Low reserves and low maintenance costs may camouflage tremendous amounts of "deferred maintenance."

Finally, brokers' setups often exaggerate potential rental rates and discount vacancies. In reality, vacancies may be much higher and the rents you can get much lower than you've been told.

In pinpointing potential returns and comparing-alternative investments, large investors, developers and financial institutions have devised further sophisticated criteria. They use comparisons taking into account the "time value" of money. Basically, they discount future cash flows by the cash-on-cash return they're seeking, to arrive at the price they will pay for any investment. Any number of other variables can be fed into their calculations. But these complex methods are far from foolproof — especially if their basic assumptions about a project and the economy in general are wrong in the first place.

Projecting annual increases of a certain percentage based on inflation is another typical and potentially devastating mistake. There's no guarantee that real estate values in general will match inflation on a step for step basis. The match is even harder to predict for individual properties.

Samuel Zell, a leading critic of the "numbers crunchers" analysis of real estate investment, says their approach "reflects a naivete that only can lead to disaster." Rather than focus on numerical indexes, Zell says, investors should focus on the "unique characteristics that protect the investment from competition."[22]

But if you consider the three overlooked elements of return mentioned above — *appreciation, equity buildup and tax effects* — you'll already be far ahead of most investors. A study by the U.S. Department of Housing and Urban Development found that few investors even looked beyond the average cash-on-cash return in evaluating their investments.[23] The same could probably be said for most Canadian real estate investors. But that's no excuse for being among the uninformed majority.

CHAPTER 4

Mortgage Financing

Do mortgages intimidate you? Do you fear the weight of debt they signify hanging over your head like the Sword of Damocles? Are you happiest living "free and clear?" "No debt, no worry," you say. That's fine — if you're a pension fund or an insurance company. But if you're an individual and you want to create real estate riches, the fastest way is by carefully using borrowed money in the form of mortgage loans.

For a real estate investor, a mortgage is not a burden. It's a tool of the business. Basically, it provides leverage, allowing you to control relatively large assets with relatively small amounts of your own money, maybe even none. And in contrast to other common investments — not to mention personal debts — real estate can carry the cost of the loan you use to buy it, while providing you with a return on your own cash investment.

A carpenter has his saws and planes, a lawyer his library, the surgeon his hospital. The real estate investor has his mortgages. But as with any tools of the trade, whether mechanical or abstract, the real estate investor's tools are useless without knowledge. Used carelessly, borrowed money can wound you grievously in the pocketbook. Used wisely, it can help make you rich.

Overall, Canadians don't seem to be excessively concerned with mortgage debt. Collectively, we owe more than $276 billion in mortgage debt. That's about $103,000 each for every man, woman and child in the country.[24]

Despite their widespread use, there is still a lot of confusion as to exactly what mortgages are and how they work.

To put them in context, mortgages are part of property law, which is ultimately rooted in English Common Law, going back before the Norman Conquest in 1066. Common Law is the ever changing body of laws built up from judicial opinions. In addition, it is modified

22

from time to time by statute law — laws passed by federal and provincial legislatures.

The exception is Quebec, where property law is controlled by the *Civil Code*. But for the purposes of real estate investment, the principles of using *hypothecs* instead of mortgages are identical. Indeed, in the real estate business, the trend has been to replace Civil Law terms with words familiar to people in the rest of the country.

A mortgage is simply a transfer of an interest in real property from the party who owns that interest to one who doesn't. (Real property is land and the improvements on it, such as buildings. By contrast, personal property includes such things as bank accounts and moveable items such as furniture or appliances in a house.)

The party transferring the interest is the *mortgagor*, the party receiving it is the *mortgagee*. In Land Titles, a mortgage is a charge, a mortgagor is a chargor and a mortgagee is a chargee.

Usually the transfer is from a borrower to a lender; and in that case the mortgagor gets the money, the lender gets the mortgage. And any value left in the property above the amount of the mortgage loan(s) is commonly called *equity* and belongs to the mortgagor.

So when people say they have a mortgage on their property, what they really mean is that they have *given* a mortgage on their property to someone else and in return they've usually gotten money. We say *usually*, because in some situations you might, for instance, exchange a mortgage on one property for an interest in another one or to secure another obligation or for estate or marriage contract planning.

Sources of Mortgage Loan Funds
- *institutions*, including life insurance companies chartered banks and their mortgage loan subsidiaries, trust companies, credit unions, caisses populaires, mortgage loan companies, treasury offices and pension funds.
- *private sources*, mainly private investors and private corporations. If you have sufficient RRSP funds, you can even be your own lender. Your self-directed RRSP can advance you mortgage money as long as the loan is insured and administered independently.
- *direct government lending*, mainly through the Canada Mortgage and Housing Corporation (CMHC).
- *vendor financing*, in which the seller of a property facilitates the sale by taking back part of the purchase price in the form of one or more mortgages.

Encumbrances
Any property can have a number of mortgages registered against it, as well as other claims. These are all called encumbrances. If the mortgagor/borrower fails to keep his obligations under any of these encum-

brances, the mortgagee/lender may choose to take legal action to possess and possibly sell the property interest that is security for his loan. He does this by way of *foreclosure, power of sale* or *judicial sale.* These encumbrances are:

- *municipal taxes*, which have first priority above and beyond all other claims. This is why institutional lenders often insist on collecting the taxes from the property owner along with the monthly mortgage payment or, alternatively, getting a receipted tax bill each year.
- *condominium fees*, which in several provinces have second priority; and again, mortgagees often collect these monthly along with taxes and mortgage payments.
- *mortgages*, which come next in priority. And which mortgage comes first is a matter of when it's registered at the local Land Titles or Registry office. The first one registered is the first mortgage, the second the second and so forth.
- *conditional sales liens*, which arise when you buy an item under a conditional sales contract; e.g., a furnace or water heater. These liens are always against the item, never the real property. In the case of nonpayment, the lien holder has the right to remove the item from the property.
- *construction liens* (also called mechanics, builder's or contractor's liens), which are registered by suppliers of goods or construction services to the property. Construction liens registered before a mortgage have priority over that mortgage to the extent of the money advanced. In a building under construction, different rules apply. These may give the construction lien holder the right to register a lien a certain number of days after the work is completed. Each province has different rules on these liens.
- *judgments*, which arise from other legal actions against the property owner, can have priority over later mortgages.
- *leases* made before mortgages have priority. So that even if the borrower defaults and the lender gets the property, the tenant cannot be evicted.

Every mortgage is a unique combination of certain basics. Once you know what they are and how they interact, you can work out the available combination that best suits your own situation.

It's important to know the considerations from both sides — from the mortgagor/borrower's point of view and from that of the mortgagee/lender. Inevitably, when you become an active real estate investor, you'll be filling both roles.

Term and Amortization
All mortgages run for a fixed length of time, called the term; provide

for a repayment schedule, called *amortization*; usually bear interest; and may have any number of special privileges or restrictions.

Term

Term is the length of time the mortgage loan runs before all the principal and interest are due and payable. The end of the term is called the *maturity date*. At maturity, the mortgage/borrower may pay off or reduce the loan balance outstanding and then renew the mortgage with the mortgagee/lender or with another lender.

Currently almost all institutional mortgages for residential properties range from six months to five years. This includes both owner-occupied properties and rental buildings. Several institutions are offering seven- and ten-year mortgages.

However, home mortgages rarely exceed the five-year period because of the federal *Interest Act*. The Act allows noncorporate borrowers to pay off the entire amount of principal outstanding on mortgages of longer than five years after the expiration of five years, provided the borrower pays the mortgagee three months' interest.

Despite the availability of longer terms, there are many occasions when the investor and homeowner are better off going short-term. Short-term mortgages may be advisable when you plan on selling the property at the end of the term. In a period of stable or declining interest rates, a free and clear property gives you greater flexibility in structuring the sale. Also, if you are planning to draw equity from the property through increased mortgage financing, there's no point locking yourself into long-term financing.

Flexibility, too, is the attraction of six-month and one- or two-year *open* mortgages. In an open mortgage, you can make prepayments or switch out of the mortgage altogether at the monthly payment date with no penalty. The rates are ¼ to 1% higher than for closed mortgages, but the freedom can be invaluable.

Amortization

Amortization is simply the paying off of the mortgage debt through periodic payments. The amortization period is the length of time it would take you to discharge the mortgage loan entirely if you continued making the same payments you initially agreed to. Because most mortgage loans are for relatively large amounts, the amortization period of a mortgage is usually much longer than its term. If it weren't, few property owners could afford to make their mortgage payments. But as a real estate investor, your aim is to increase your overall equity and/or cash flow. Paying off a mortgage is usually a low priority.

Most new mortgages provide for *blended* payments — payments made in equal monthly amounts combining both principal and interest. Because the outstanding principal is constantly being reduced, with each payment the portion going towards interest decreases and the portion going towards principal increases.

Here's an example of how this works — in this case with a $50,000 blended-payment mortgage bearing interest at 13% a year compounded semi-annually and amortized over 25 years. The term doesn't affect the calculation.

TABLE 5

Payment No.	Total Payment	Interest Payment	Principal Payment	Balance of Loan
1	$551.20	$527.55	$ 23.65	$49,976.35
2	551.20	527.30	23.90	49,952.45
3	551.20	527.05	24.15	49,928.30
100	551.20	484.36	64.77	46,037.88
200	551.20	360.28	190.92	33,954.99
300	551.20	5.83	545.37	7.63
301	7.71	.08	7.63	.00

Until the nineteenth year of the life of the mortgage, each payment contains a greater portion of principal than interest because the principal is being reduced so gradually. Because the loan is amortized over such a long period — 25 years — the principal repayment is very slight in the early years of the mortgage

If the above mortgage were to run on the same terms for the full amortization period, the borrower would repay a total of $ 115,275.56 in interest for the $50,000 loan. By reducing the amortization period, the borrower can save thousands of dollars in interest.

For instance, cutting the amortization to 20 years would save $8,925.39 in interest; cutting it to 10 years would chop interest costs to $59,947.43. Of course, the monthly payments would have to be increased. For a 20-year amortization, the monthly payment would rise to $573.77; for 10 years, it would be $736.60. But as long as the borrower can afford the bigger monthly payments, the savings are hard to beat.

Besides blended payments, mortgages can provide for:

1. Flat payments or *interest-only payments* — As the name suggests, only interest is paid during the term of the mortgage. This is actually an unamortized mortgage, as you are not making any payments of principal.

2. Fixed payments of principal, often in conjunction with interest payments. The combined payments continually diminish as the mortgage principal is paid down.

3. Graduated payments, which will include principal and interest or interest only, according to the formula of the particular lender and the trend of interest rates.

Graduated payment mortgages (GPMs) were promoted by Canada Mortgage and Housing Corporation from 1981-1983 as a refuge for interest-rate shocked homeowners who couldn't afford to carry the new high rates on their home mortgages. In the initial stage of a GPM loan, the borrower actually *builds up* debt rather than paying it down. GPMs never caught on and are virtually nonexistent today.

As a matter of convenience and custom, payments under these plans have usually been made monthly. But other variations are possible. Two that have caught on are *bi-weekly* and *weekly-pay* mortgages.

Making payments more frequently effectively shortens the loan amortization period. And, as mentioned before, the quicker a mortgage loan is paid off, the less interest the borrower has to pay. The savings can be huge, as witness the effect on a $50,000 mortgage amortized over 25 years at 13%. By making payments weekly instead of monthly, you would pay the loan off in just 16 years and nine months at a savings of $45,581 in interest.

If a lender doesn't offer these options, you can get the same savings by shortening the amortization period when you negotiate the loan. The maximum amortization is usually 30 years. But you can reduce it as much as you can afford — to one year if you want, though some lenders won't go below five years.

Interest Calculation

The interest rate you're quoted on a mortgage loan usually doesn't tell you how much interest you're really paying (or receiving). Unless the mortgage is compounded annually, the *nominal* interest rate will be exceeded by the *effective* rate of interest. The difference is a result of compounding.

Say interest on your mortgage loan is compounded twice-yearly. This means that after six months, you're charged interest on the balance outstanding at half the yearly rate; however, the interest is left to accumulate as if it were another loan and you pay interest on it too. For those with a taste for algebra, there are a number of books detailing the mathematics of mortgage calculations

But the basic rule is that *the more frequently interest is compounded, the higher the effective interest rate.* For instance, a loan with a nominal interest rate of 10% compounded semi-annually actually carries an effective annual interest rate of 10.25%.

Most Canadian residential first mortgages are compounded semi-annually. But lenders can and frequently do compound *collateral mortgages* monthly. (A collateral mortgage is simply a mortgage made to secure a promissory note; and it's usually a second mortgage.) But no matter how frequently mortgage interest is calculated, the Federal *Interest Act* stipulates that, if it's a blended-payment mortgage, the lender must disclose the rate *as if it were* calculated yearly or half-yearly, not in advance.

Most mortgage loans carry a fixed rate of interest for their entire term. However, variable-rate mortgages (VRMs) are also available, though they account for fewer than 5% of residential mortgages. In a VRM, the interest rate is adjusted on a monthly basis in accord with a reference rate chosen by the lender.

If you choose a VRM mortgage loan, your monthly payment remains the same, but the amortization period is adjusted. So, for instance, if you take out a one-year VRM with a 25-year amortization period and the interest rate rises that year, you will have paid off very little of the principal amount you borrowed. If interest rates drop, you'll be ahead: the amortization period will be shortened, so you'll be paying off a greater amount of principal.

Nevertheless, most observers feel that the main beneficiaries of VRMs are the lenders. By going the VRM route, institutions that would otherwise borrow short-term and lend long-term decrease their uncertainty.

Privileges and Restrictions
These elements with every mortgage can be just as important as the other elements.

Prepayment privileges allow you to reduce the outstanding principal. And the more principal you pay off, the lower are your interest charges. Every lender has different policies. The most liberal policies are attached to *open* mortgages, in which you can pay off all or part of the principal at specified times during the term of the mortgage, usually on the monthly payment date.

Mortgage-rate protection offered by several lenders gives you some of the flexibility of an open mortgage on a *closed* mortgage. For example, if your mortgage is at 12% and you believe rates will soon rise sharply, you may want to switch into a three-year mortgage at, say 11%. Lenders charge a fee *and* the dollar difference between your current rate and the new rate (if the new rate is lower) for the balance of the existing mortgage term.

Prepayment privileges on otherwise closed mortgages are a big selling point for many lenders. Various "10 plus 10" plans, for instance, allow you to pay off 10% of the principal once a year and to increase your monthly payments once a year by as much as 10% without penalty. One bank permits you to as much as double your regular monthly payments and then add a further amount equal to the original monthly payment. But once you increase your regular monthly payment, you are stuck with it for the term of the mortgage. Another lender's VRM allows $100 minimum prepayments without charge, and lets you discharge the entire loan for a $200 administrative charge.

However, mortgage loan defaults in the last recession have stiffened lenders' standards in other matters. And you can hardly blame them as their own debt obligations undergo round after round of credit agency downgrading.

Today, mortgages are rarely automatically assumable. Just because you sell a property doesn't mean the mortgage goes along with it. Probably, most mortgages can be assumed only if the new buyer meets with the lender's approval. And that approval may be "unreasonably withheld." Many mortgages also contain "due on sale" clauses. In other words, when the property is sold, the mortgage loan comes due. What if the mortgage is closed, contains an approval clause and the lender won't approve the buyer? The answer is a simple "no sale." Sometimes, though, the lender may have doubts about the new buyer, but will still approve the sale, reasoning that he can always go back against the original borrower/ mortgagor if there's a problem.

In any case, if you're selling a property on which you took out a mortgage loan that's being assigned, remember that *until a mortgage is discharged, the lender always has the right to go against the original mortgagor under the "personal covenant" in the mortgage.* Usually, the lender won't do so if the realized value of the property exceeds its losses on a default. But if the lender is still out money, it can and will go after the original borrower.

To entice homeowners to switch lenders when their current mortgage term is up, some lenders are offering free mortgage transfers. But you may have to pay a fee to the lender you're leaving.

Though there have been few takers, a federal Mortgage Rate Protection Plan applicable to first mortgages taken out or renewed after 1 March 1984 is still available. For a fee equal to 1.5% of the mortgage, Ottawa agrees to pick up 75% of extra interest costs — *not counting the first two percentage points* — if the rate rises at the end of the initial term. However, the plan is limited to a maximum increase of 12 percentage points above the initial rate on your mortgage for a maximum $70,000 mortgage; there is no minimum term. The protection applies for a term equal to the initial term. Overall, the protection is so minimal though and the cost so high that the plan has attracted only 81 borrowers.

Finding the Right Combination

When weighing investment alternatives, you may have to choose among various combinations of mortgages. How do you put them on a common basis? One approach is to average the mortgages. The formula is:

$$\frac{\text{Amount of first} \times \text{interest rate of first} \ + \ \text{Amount of second} \times \text{interest rate of second}}{\text{Total amount being financed}}$$

If there are more than two mortgages, add them to the numerator. This formula calculates the total amount of interest paid for a year as an expression of the total amount of money borrowed.

For instance, say the first mortgage is $100,000 at 12%, and the second $50,000 at 14%. The calculation is:

$$\frac{\$100,000 \times 12\% \ + \ \$50,000 \times 14\%}{\$150,000} \ =$$

$$\frac{\$12,000 \times 7,000}{\$150,000} \ =$$

$$\frac{\$19,000}{\$150,000} \ =$$

.1266%

But looking at interest rates alone won't give you a full comparison of financing alternatives. For instance, if the mortgages expire at different times, the averaging can't account for the new rate(s). Averaging also tells you nothing about special restrictions or privileges, monthly payments and amortization periods.

Other Points to Consider

*   *Application fees* — Competition among lenders has narrowed price differences. But be sure to check whether the application fee also includes the cost of the required appraisal.
*   *How are the realty taxes paid?* — Many lenders divide the estimated taxes by 12, add that amount to your monthly payment and then pay the municipality directly. This ensures that the taxes are paid. But because they pay them either two or six times a year, your "tax account" with the lender almost always has an "excess" or a "deficiency." On the excess you're often paid from zero to 3% interest; on the deficiency, you're charged the bank's prime rate, plus.
*   *Legal fees* — Will the lender accept certification of title and preparation of the mortgage documents by your lawyer? If not, you could end up paying legal fees twice. *Get the lender's acceptance in writing so there is no misunderstanding.*
*   *Discharge fees* — Some lenders do not charge you for preparing and registering a discharge of your mortgage, while others take

advantage of this opportunity for quick profit. A discharge is usually only a matter of filling in several blanks on a one-page form, then paying the registry office $25 to $50 for registration. Yet lenders — and in private mortgages, lawyers — regularly charge up to $200 for this.

CHAPTER 5

How to Come Up a Winner When Applying for Mortgage Money

Know Your Lender
Recently an investor applied to a major trust company for a $20,000 second mortgage loan on his own home. He planned to use the money to renovate several of his investment properties. The investor was single, earned $35,000 a year, had a top credit rating and each of his properties carried itself. Aside from the first mortgage loan on his home, he had no personal debts. Yet he was turned down flat.

Why?

First, the company said his monthly costs exceeded their guidelines by 2%.

Secondly, they asked what would happen if all his rental properties became vacant? How could he continue to pay the mortgages and taxes on them with the added burden of a $20,000 second mortgage?

The flabbergasted investor finally did obtain his financing — and $40,000 more — from a second institution. And he used neither magic nor deception to get it. The manager and the institution were simply more receptive to property investment. And the investor dealt directly with the branch manager, not with a clerk as he had at the trust company.

What lessons can the small real estate investor learn from this?

Know your lender and plan ahead. Know what lenders are looking for, what they're avoiding and what they expect. Don't just wander into the nearest bank or trust company, pour out your financial history to the bored clerk and expect to get the loan you need on the terms you want.

Qualifying for a Loan
How do you qualify for a loan for your own home? Public lenders such as banks, trust companies, credit unions and life insurance

31

companies use two ratios: Gross Debt Service (GDS) and Total Debt Service (TDS).

The Gross Debt Service ratio refers to the percentage of your monthly gross income that will go towards payments for mortgage principal, interest and taxes (PIT). Lenders generally insist on a 30% maximum ratio. When funds are tight or lenders want to cut their risk, they'll chop the ratio to 25% or even lower. Some lenders however use a higher ratio, up to 34%, but include in it an estimate of your monthly utility costs. In the case of spouses buying a home, both incomes are counted.

For instance, if your gross yearly income is $40,000, you could afford to spend $1,000 a month for PIT ($40,000 x 30% divided by 12). Subtract $100 a month for taxes (or whatever amount is appropriate to the price of homes in your area) and you're left with $900 for principal and interest payments. That's enough to afford about $100,500 in mortgaging for a 10% first mortgage for one year amortized over 25 years.

To calculate your mortgage level, you can refer to books of monthly mortgage tables, including mortgage value and mortgage outstanding tables, which are available at any large bookstore. Be sure, though, that you buy a book compounding interest in the Canadian manner. The same applies to computer programs.

To calculate your current GDS, just divide your PIT by your gross annual income. Don't be surprised if your GDS exceeds 30%. According to institutional guidelines, many homeowners can't afford the homes they have been living in and carrying for years.

Besides looking at your GDS and down payment, lenders also will calculate your Total Debt Service ratio. The TDS ratio is the percentage of your total gross monthly income that goes towards all your monthly debts, including PIT and all consumer loan payments.

Expressed as a formula, the TDS ratio is PIT + loan payments divided by income. Say you want to buy a home with existing financing and taxes calling for x dollars a year. Simply add that figure to your other monthly consumer debts and divide the total by your gross annual income (TDS = PIT + loan payments divided by income).

So if the PIT is $750 and you're paying, say, $200 a month in car installments and $100 on your VISA card, your monthly costs are $1,050 or $12,600 a year. Divide the $12,600 by your yearly gross income of say, $40,000, thus giving you a TDS of 31.5%.

Most lenders set a maximum TDS of 40% to 42%. Interestingly, some lenders *assume* a TDS ratio of 40% even if you have *never* incurred consumer debts. So while you may qualify on a GDS basis, you could still be turned down for the loan.

But meeting the GDS and TDS ratios is only part of the story. You still must have at least 25% of the purchase price in a cash down payment in order to qualify for a *conventional* mortgage. If not, you will have to arrange mortgage insurance. A mortgage loan covering more than 75% of the purchase price is a *high-ratio loan*. And if it's from an institution, it must be insured by law — either through the private Mortgage Insurance Company of Canada (MICC) or Canada Mortgage and Housing Corporation (CMHC).

Even if your loan is not high-ratio, institutional lenders look into the *entire* financing on the purchase. So, for instance, if vendor-take-back mortgages reduce your down payment — or raise your GDS and TDS ratios unacceptably — the lender may not make the loan. Even though its mortgage loan may be fully secured, as far as loan to value ratio, institutional lenders don't want the costs and responsibilities of realizing their security.

Some buyers avoid the lenders' scrutiny by arranging to advance a mortgage to the seller shortly after closing. But circumventing safeguards can be dangerous. In the 1990–93 recession, residential real estate prices in Toronto plunged an average 35% from their pre-recession heights. This massive erasure of equity saw homeowners walking away from properties, private mortgage holders stuck with valueless paper and smaller lenders shut down abruptly by the province.

Other factors lenders consider before making the loan include the following:

1. Source of your down payment — Lenders understandably frown on a borrowed down payment in the case of a novice investor or homeowner. With none of your own money at risk in a property, you'll have less incentive to keep up the payments if the going gets rough.

2. Reliability and stability of your income — How long have you been employed? What portion of your income is from bonuses? Commissions? Special incentives?

3. How much reliance you have on supplementary and spouse's income — Steady part-time work by either spouse can bring your income up to required levels. However, depending on the nature of the income, only a portion will be used in the calculation. Capital gains or other extraordinary income will usually not be included at all.

Paying off your consumer debts from savings can also help you by reducing your TDS ratio to acceptable levels. In any case, paying high interest on non-tax deductible consumer debt doesn't make much sense if you have the money to pay it off anyway.

Financing Small Investment Properties
Qualifying for loans for small investment properties requires more

persistence and planning. To begin with, some institutions won't even consider an application for a mortgage loan for a rental house. And if they do, it will often come with a variety of conditions. For example, they may assume the house will remain vacant and that you will have to support it out of your regular income. They may require mortgage insurance. And even then the lender may withhold all or part of its advance until you can show a signed lease for the premises. The lender may insist on this before you even take possession of the property. In other words, you may have to prove the property is rented before you even own it. As well, lenders may charge a higher interest rate than if the mortgage loan were for a principal residence. And they may shorten the amortization period from the 25 years that most people are accustomed to, to 20 years or less. They may also cut the percentage of property value they will finance. Instead of financing 75% of appraised value, they may only advance 50% to 70%.

Their appraisals, too, may be unrealistically low. Most institutions don't use professionally qualified appraisers to determine value. They use what are more properly termed "mortgage inspectors." These inspectors know what you propose paying for the property and they make sure their employers won't be lending you more than the percentage of that price they want. Some lenders are notorious for this practice; none are immune.

In light of these restrictions, it's not surprising that small investors have been known to buy properties for their own use, but then "change their minds" and rent them out. Though the lenders can terminate the loan if they find out, they usually don't bother to check — provided they receive their mortgage payments on time and you pay the taxes.

When you're dealing with institutional lenders you should also keep these points in mind:

- Lots of information is traded among the local credit bureaus. So don't fudge what can be found out.
- Be aware that every time you make an application for credit, it is recorded by the local credit reporting agency. If you are turned down by one lender, the next one will know about it. Subsequent lenders you approach will then know that either: 1) you have been turned down for credit, which will make them leery of your application; or, 2) you are shopping around for credit, which will also make them suspect your sincerity and creditworthiness. Thus when you make an application with a lender, you should be as certain as you can that you will meet their underwriting standards and that you can document everything they will ask of you.
- There's no need to volunteer information to lenders that they can't find out if you don't tell them. For instance, say you own a half-

dozen homes which you rent out, all financed with vendor-take-back mortgages. You then apply for an institutional loan for a new property. Proud of your track record with investment properties, you tell the lenders about them. But the lender may well see your accomplishments another way: as a half-dozen liabilities that could jeopardize its receiving its payments. Result: application denied. And now all other lenders too will know about those "liabilities."

CHAPTER 6

The High-Ratio Mortgage and Alternatives

How much can you borrow against a property to buy it? Institutional lenders are strictly bound to lending limits based on your equity in the property. Any mortgage for up to 75% of value is considered a *conventional* mortgage. Any mortgage for more than 75% of value is called a *high-ratio mortgage*. With the exception of first-time buyers, the highest loan-to-value ratio (LTV) allowed is 90%. Only mortgage loans for owner-occupied and rental housing are eligible for mortgage insurance.

If you're getting a high-ratio mortgage loan from an institution, you have to insure it so that in case you default, the lender will recover its money. Though you pay for the insurance, it's the lender who is compensated. The aim is to protect the general public that has its funds in the institutions. Private lenders and vendors with no money from the general public aren't bound to these limits and can't get their mortgages insured.

Mortgage brokers are frequently involved with mortgage insurance applications. However, you *do not need the help of a mortgage broker or any other intermediary to apply for mortgage insurance*. You can apply for insurance directly with the institutional lender you're borrowing from.

This type of insured mortgage shouldn't be confused with life insured mortgage, where, for a fee based on your age and the insured amount, your loan is repaid if you, or your spouse, die before the mortgage is discharged. Each lender is affiliated with an insurer it chooses, so rates and terms vary as much as 50%. One of the lower cost arrangements is through the Toronto Dominion Bank, where you can insure up to $300,000 in residential mortgages ($500,000 if you meet the insurer's medical criteria) on as many properties as you need to, *including investment properties*. Fees per $1,000 of mortgage range from 8¢ (11¢ including spouse) for borrowers 28 and younger, to

52¢ and 84¢ at age 55 and $1.64 and $2.46 at age 69. The combined rate is based on the age of the eldest spouse.

First Home Loan Insurance
In February 1992, CMHC introduced a two-year "initiative" to make homebuying more affordable. CMHC's rationale was that many people could afford monthly carrying costs, but were stymied by insufficient cash for down payments. The solution was First Home Loan Insurance, a 5% down payment plan for first-time homebuyers only. To qualify, buyers must use the home as their principal residence and must not have owned a principal residence at any time during the previous five years. If there is a co-buyer, only one has to be a first-time buyer. Buyers must insure the mortgage with either CMHC or the only other Canadian mortgage insurer, privately owned MICC.

To qualify for the plan, you must spend no more than 35% of your gross family income on principal, interest, property taxes and heating. Your total debt load can't exceed 42% of your gross family income (see Chapter 8). The insurance premium is 2.5% of the loan, 3% if there are multiple advances; the premium can be added to the mortgage. The minimum mortgage term is five years.

There is a general $250,000 price ceiling on homes in the greater Toronto and Vancouver areas. Another 20 areas have a $175,000 ceiling. All other areas are restricted to a $125,000 maximum. For verification of current limits, check with your local CMHC office.

Ottawa predicted that 10,000 households would take advantage of the program in its first year. But in the first three months alone, 26,000 applications were approved nationwide under the plan. In the first half of 1991, the plan helped boost first-time home purchases to 49% of all sales in Montreal, and more than half in Toronto. A large portion of first-time buyers were spending only 25% of their income on carrying costs, indicating that they weren't overreaching to make the purchase. This may calm concerns by some analysts who recall a similar 5%-down payment plan in the early 1970s (AHOP) that saw thousands of homeowners walk away from their homes when interest rates rose. Nevertheless, a spokesman for MICC says the plan created a "major issue of risk" for the insurers. He points out that only one lender puts in an "approval" clause for the insurance to be transferred to a subsequent buyer. And, in MICC's experience, 70% of mortgage defaults are by subsequent buyers. Depending on the circumstances of the sale, the insurer may go after the original insured for any losses arising from a subsequent buyer defaulting.

If you're not a first-time homebuyer, you'll need at least a 10% down payment. If you're buying or building an investment property, you'll need at least a 15% down payment. That down payment can't be borrowed. You'll be asked to show its source. Acceptable sources are: *bona fide* savings, an agreement for the sale of a home, sale of stocks, GIC certificates, outright gifts documented by the donor, government grants and, in restricted circumstances, "sweat" equity and rent as equity. Credit checks the lender uses will reveal any institutional loans, so don't try padding your "savings" with credit card advances, as one late-night real estate guru used to advocate. However, it is acceptable to use as equity, borrowings against other assets; payments on those loans will be taken into consideration in calculating your mortgage eligibility.

There's no maximum amount for insured mortgage loans. However, to cover the house or duplex you live in, both insurers require at least 20% cash for the balance of the purchase price exceeding $180,000. In other words, you can insure 90% of the first $180,000 and 80% of the balance. So, on a $200,000 home, for example, you can only insure $178,000 of the mortgage financing.

Thus,

$$90\% \times \$180,000 = \$162,000$$
$$80\% \times \$\ 20,000 = \underline{\$\ 16,000}$$
$$\$178,000$$

Where the down payment is 10% or less, the premium is 2.5%; with up to 15% down, the premium is 2%; up to 20% down, you're charged 1.25% and with up to 25% down, the premium drops to ¾%. CMHC is tougher on variable rate mortgages: it drops the maximum to 85% and boosts the premium ¼%. Lenders on investment or expensive estate properties may insist you insure conventional mortgages. Both insurers charge premiums of ½% as long as you have at least 35% down.

For full processing, meaning application and appraisal, both insurers charge $235. As well, lenders charge their own fees for application (and sometimes appraisal) — which together range from $25 to as much as $250.

On investment properties, the maximum LTV is 85%, which applies regardless of the amount insured. For a one- to three-unit building, MICC charges the same premiums and up-front fees, whether you live in the building or not. Other rates are on a case-by-case basis. CMHC premiums on one- to four-unit buildings are the same as your home as long as you live in the building; LTV is up to 90%. On rental properties with LTV up to 85%, the premium is 1.5-2% for existing buildings, and up to 3% for new rental properties.

Second mortgages can also be insured. But as the premium is based on the *total* amount of the first and second mortgages, the premium is high in relation to the mortgage amount.

To make up for the tremendous underwriting losses that marred both the beginning and end of the last decade, insurance fees rose drastically in the late '80s and aren't likely to come down soon.

Consequently, today high-ratio insurance is not always the first choice for financing the purchase of property with little money down.

Whether the property is mortgaged or clear, vendor-take-back mortgages offer workable alternatives. Instead of placing a high-cost, high-ratio insured mortgage on the property, the vendor agrees to take back one or two mortgages. Then he sells one or both to a mortgage broker, or directly to an investor if he can. The discount is usually less than the cost of insuring and processing a new high-ratio institutional mortgage. The key to working out an alternative to the high-ratio mortgage is to lower the overall financing costs. Effectively, the buyer and seller then split the savings one way or another.

In considering alternatives to high-ratio financing, as a buyer you should also remember that short-term vendor-take-back mortgages will have to be renewed and the cost and rates have to be balanced against the benefits of an insured first mortgage.

CHAPTER 7

Vendor-Take-Back Mortgages

Both buyers and sellers can profit from vendor take back (VTB) mortgages. (In Quebec, VTBs are called "balance of sale," but are essentially the same)[27] If the seller is willing to go the VTB route, the property can often be more readily sold since financing is immediately available. Buyers usually get better mortgage terms than they could get from institutions, and sellers get well-secured investments with potential tax benefits.

Another lure of VTBs is their flexibility. Seller financing facilitates the creation of terms and conditions most exactly suited to the particular situation. Neither party is bound to any of the set formulas that control institutional lending.

For the buyer, VTB financing is almost always preferable to institutional financing — and that applies whether you're talking about a multi-million dollar office building or a modest condominium apartment.

Advantages to the Borrower

- *Low interest rates* — Seller financing is almost always at a lower rate than institutional financing. This is especially true for second or subsequent mortgages. In contrast to the institutional lender, the seller's main goal is selling the property. Squeezing a few dollars more out of the financing isn't usually much of a concern. (In special situations, however, it is in the *buyer's* interest to pay an above-average interest rate. See below, *Splitting the Amount.*)

- *Special privileges* — such as the right of prepayment — can be negotiated. In commercial transactions, it's not unusual for arrangements to be made for delayed payments. This may happen where the buyer has to carry a vacant or semi-vacant building for several months until it is renovated and rented. In another twist, an investor recently bought out his co-owner's interest in a property. Rather than pay cash (that he didn't have anyway), he gave back a one-year "balloon" mortgage, with no payments of principal or interest due until one year from the date of the sale.

- *Low down payment* — The down payment may be lower than that required by an institution.
- *Credit checking* isn't as stringent as with an institutional lender.

Indeed, it is the exception rather than the rule for home sellers to even ask for information on the buyer, let alone run a proper credit check. For his first few house investments, one impecunious investor purposely looked only for properties on which the seller was willing to take back financing.

But just because an institution won't accept certain borrowers doesn't mean they're bad credit risks. For instance, buyers with big down payments can sometimes demonstrate only a limited income, and thus can't qualify for institutional financing.

Even declared income doesn't always impress institutional lenders. Banks and large trust companies typically refuse to count several years of substantial capital gains as income. This isn't "real" income, they say, since there's no guarantee that it can be obtained again. They prefer a borrower with a steady job; apparently they have never heard of unemployment.

- *Prompt answers* — When the seller is agreeable to taking back the mortgage, you can make a firm offer. You don't have to wait for an okay from the lender.
- *Lower placement costs* — The seller won't take an application fee, demand a new survey or ask for an independent appraisal.

Benefits for the Seller

Taking back all or part of the financing makes your property more saleable. For example, by adjusting the terms of the mortgages, you can match the buyer's payments to his ability to pay. You can also tie up a sale faster than if the buyer were to seek outside financing, as you can give practically instant approval.

Also, VTB mortgages are relatively liquid — they can usually be converted to cash quickly.

You can sell a VTB mortgage, or, in a financial version of having your cake and eating it too, you can use a VTB as security against other loans.

Keeping your VTB mortgage instead of selling it has many advantages too. First, you won't have to pay broker's fees and/or discounts incurred in selling outface that can eat up as much as 50% of the face value of the mortgage. Second, the mortgage is secured by a "hard" asset, i.e., the property, that can be sold to recoup the value of the loan if the borrower defaults. Last, the return is often higher than you would get from an institutional investment.

42

Interest from VTB mortgages must be reported as income. Though private mortgage investing is a popular ploy with aspiring tax evaders, the risks are high. To begin with, there is a clear paper trail. Furthermore, the borrowers often deduct the interest as a business expense to legitimately reduce their taxable incomes. So, if Revenue Canada asks them for verification of their expenses, the private lender (and his "oversights") are in the spotlight.

Drawbacks for Lenders
There's no downside for the VTB-borrower. But if you're a lender, there can be drawbacks both obvious and hidden. There's always the risk of *default*, where the borrower doesn't make his payments, and *default loss*, where you can't get back your losses by selling the property or enforcing a judgment against the defaulting borrower.

Also, as usual, there are tax considerations. The first arises where you take back a mortgage upon selling your own home, leaving yourself short of the money you need for your new home. So you could end up paying in taxes up to 50% of the interest you're earning on your VTB. Meanwhile, the interest you're paying on your new home will not be tax deductible. In that situation, it might be better to take the loss on selling the mortgage than holding the VTB.

Secondly, in deciding whether or not to take back a mortgage on a sale giving rise to taxable gains, you should consider how "reserve" provisions can lower your taxes. Where you don't realize the total profit on resale all at once, you are normally allowed to spread the gain over a maximum of five years, but at least 20% of the gain must be recognized in the year of disposition.

Forms of VTB Mortgage Financing
VTB mortgages can take any of the forms found in institutional mortgages. But here are the most common variations and features of VTB financing:

Open Privileges
Open privileges allow all or any part of the principal to be repaid at any time or times without notice or bonus. Alternatively, principal repayments may be limited to a certain percentage or dollar amount at specified times. Or you may close the mortgage for a period and open it later. For example, you might take back a five-year mortgage at a certain rate of interest with the first two years closed and the final three years open.

Splitting the Amount
Splitting the amount taken back into two or more mortgages is a common solution where the seller wants to facilitate the sale, but still needs

to draw money out of the property as a down payment on a new property of his own. Dividing the amount enables the seller to sell one or more of the mortgages — and thus realize a lump-sum cash payment — while still offering an inducement to the buyer. If the cost (discount) of selling the mortgage is unacceptable, you could consider taking a personal loan from an institution or an individual investor using the mortgage as collateral. If the interest on the loan is less than the discount, it may be a better choice.

Before making your decision, be sure also to look at the tax considerations. The discount will probably be treated as a capital loss, which can only be used to offset capital gains. But the interest on the loan is normally fully deductibles long as it's used with the intent and reasonable expectation of generating income.

The discount on selling the mortgage depends on:
1) The creditworthiness of the buyer.
2) The property itself.
3) The term of the mortgage.
4) The face rate of interest.
5) Special privileges.

The lower the rate and the longer the term (if the face rate is *below* current rates), the greater the discount. In other words, whomever buys the mortgage will adjust what he pays for it so that the return he realizes will at least match what he could get by buying a similar investment. Mortgage table books enable you to easily figure out the discounts.

Open mortgages will be discounted more than closed mortgages, because at any time the loan may be discharged and the mortgage buyer will have to reinvest his money, perhaps for a lower return. Some trust companies simply won't buy any open mortgages.

The mortgage broker's fee will be added to the discount, though the entire fee will likely be quoted to you as a discount. You could also be hit for appraisal and inspection fees, as well as legal and survey costs.

In practice, the *total* cost for selling the mortgage can be up to double the discount to bring it to a market rate. But in urban areas the secondary mortgage market is highly competitive and you can save literally thousands of dollars by shopping around.

If you've split the amount of VTB financing, you can also save on the discount by adjusting the rates on the two mortgages. There's no reason a second mortgage has to be at a higher rate than a first mortgage. In fact, the reverse can benefit both parties.

Take the case where there are two VTB mortgages and the seller is to sell the first. To decrease the discount, the first should be at a high rate, or even above current institutional rates. But to keep the buyer's total monthly payments at an acceptable level, the rate of the second mortgage could be much lower than current rates. The seller would save on the discount while the buyer would still get the benefit of an overall lower mortgage payment than he would have by going the institutional route.

Over the term of the second mortgage that the buyer retains, the seller will receive less in payments than he would have otherwise. But this may still be far more than the discount he would have had to take on the mortgage he sold had he not adjusted the rates.

If the discount for selling the VTB is prohibitive no matter how you rearrange it, you could consider offering to pay down the interest rate the buyer would pay on a new high-ratio mortgage. Your savings would come from not having to pay the mortgage broker's fee and other related costs .

Low-interest VTB Mortgages
These benefit the buyer by keeping payments low while the seller eventually gets his price.

No-interest VTB Mortgages
In this kind of mortgage, only principal is repaid — no interest. Zero-interest mortgages are especially popular during periods of high interest rates. In 1982, for instance, trust companies exercising their power of sale on homes on which borrowers had defaulted sometimes made zero interest loans to buyers. This way the companies retained a higher asset value on their books than they would have had they dropped the sale price.

While the seller-lender "loses" interest, his cash flow can remain unaffected — as long as periodic repayments of principal are specified and the amortization period is sufficiently short. In other words, just because the buyer is getting an interest-free mortgage doesn't mean he can't make monthly payments on it. The difference is that none of those payments has an interest component. Instead, every dollar goes toward paying down the principal.

One caution though: if the intent of the no-interest mortgage is tax reduction, National Revenue may still assess you tax on the basis that it's an "artificial transaction," and that a portion of what you're calling capital is, in fact, interest and is taxable as such.

Long-term Mortgages
Five-year terms for home mortgages have become a standard maximum in the last 30 years. (During the high-interest-rate early-1980s, three-year terms were often the longest terms available from lenders.) But as inflation subsided and interest rates dropped, long-term mortgages started looking good.

Instead of fixing the terms of the mortgage for the entire period, you could write in an option to renew the mortgage after a fixed period at an agreed upon rate. Be sure, if you do this, that in the purchase and sale agreement you specify the renewal rate, either exactly or by reference to another rate. You could insert a clause such as "Upon termination of this mortgage, it shall be renewable on the same terms and conditions for a further period of (x) years." Or: "Upon termination, this mortgage shall be renewable on the same terms and conditions for a further period of (x) years except that the interest rate shall be (x) percentage points (above or below) the lowest fixed rate for (x) bank's homeowner loans of the same term."

Long Amortization Periods
An amortization period longer than the usual 25-year maximum of institutional mortgages could help bring the monthly payments down to a more affordable level for the buyer. For example, a $100,000 10% mortgage amortized over 25 years costs $894.49. But amortized over 30 years it costs $862.67; and for 40 years, $833.30. The downside of an extended amortization period is that you pay off very little of the principal during the early years. In the example above, during the first year the following amounts are paid off after one year: 25 year amortization, $1,000; 30 years, $600; 40 years, $200.

Other Points to Keep in Mind

1. If you're selling a VTB mortgage, get a commitment, or at least a quotation, on the discount *before* you complete the sale agreement. Virtually all mortgage brokers insist that the buyer have at least a 10% to 15% down payment, or they won't buy the mortgage. Furthermore, the buyer's down payment should not ordinarily be borrowed.

2. If you're holding the VTB mortgage, make the purchase conditional on a satisfactory check of the buyer's credit. To satisfy provincial consumer protection laws, be sure the offer includes a clause directing the buyer to give you written permission for a credit report.

3. Don't let a hefty down payment fool you into forgoing a credit check. The down payment itself may be borrowed and the buyer on the verge of financial collapse.

4. If the terms of a VTB mortgage are much more generous than those of an institutional mortgage, the seller should make the mortgage *non-transferable*. After all, you gave the buyer favorable terms to enable him to buy the property, not to give him windfall speculative gains by reselling it.

5. If there is a taxable gain on the sale, remember to allow for those taxes — either by paying them out of a sufficient down payment

or from other sources. But don't borrow to pay taxes. Interest on money borrowed to pay taxes is not deductible.

6. Many real estate agents are unfamiliar with VTB mortgages. So you'll have to be the expert. Or better yet, list or buy only through a knowledgeable agent.

CHAPTER 8

Creative Financing

Several years ago, Mary Ann, a single mother of two, was told by her landlord that, if she wanted, she could buy the house she was renting. Unfortunately, she didn't have a down payment. But as a tenant, she had been prompt with her rent payments. So, banking on the goodwill built up by that — and a certain amount of naiveté — she asked the owner to take back a mortgage for the entire purchase price at a fixed interest rate for ten years and he agreed.

Which goes to prove that sometimes the most creative financing is simply a matter of asking.

In most situations you run into as a small investor, creativity revolves around terms in the vendor-take-back mortgages. But there are also other creative, workable and honest ways of reducing or eliminating the cash you have to put into a property. Essentially, they involve 1) converting other assets you own or have access to into down payments; 2) utilizing other people's money instead of your own.

Converting Other Assets

- Assign to the vendor periodic cash payments people owe you. These could include mortgage payments, rents on other property, stock dividends and regular interest payments for such things as GICs, Canada or other government savings bonds.

  By assigning the income, rather than selling the asset outright, you reap a number of possible advantages: no tax liability on any capital gain; no transaction costs, other than the minor one of assigning the income-earning interest in the asset; and you retain the asset itself, along with the possibility of future capital gain income or use that entails.

- Use the equity in your own home as a down payment by giving the seller a first, second or third mortgage on it in lieu of a cash down payment. This is a more direct and cheaper way to draw on the equity in your home than mortgaging your property first and then using the money to invest in real estate. You avoid application, survey and appraisal fees; and the mortgage itself will usually be more flexible and bear a lower interest rate than you could otherwise get.

Many first-time home buyers borrow money from relatives for a down payment. But there's no reason they couldn't exchange mortgages on their properties for the down payment in the property being bought.

The seller may even accept chattel mortgages on personal property, particularly a car, truck or motorhome.

- Give the seller a promissory note or notes in exchange for the deposit on all or part of the down payment. This method is most useful where there's a small shortfall between an existing mortgage and your cash down payment. Rarely will a seller accept a note unaccompanied by a significant amount of cash.
- Barter other valuable assets, such as jewels, furs, stocks, bonds, motor vehicles, art or stamps for the down payment.
- Exchange the use of assets or services themselves for an interest in property. Do you have a vacation home that the seller might want to use for a summer? Or a motor boat? Or motor home or travel trailer? Do you have a profession or trade? Maybe the seller could use a new bathroom or kitchen? A paint job for his car? A divorce?

Using Other People's Money

- Ask the vendor to arrange new financing on the property, which you then agree to take over. The idea is that the new mortgage(s) may give him the cash he needs — and which you don't have. It's easier for the vendor to arrange the new mortgages than it is for you, especially if you have little or no down payment.
- Another approach is to take out demand loans and then use them either as down payments or in lieu of mortgage money.

Institutional lenders are often more comfortable with consumer expenditures than real estate investments. So novice real estate investors sometimes start off borrowing money for, say, a vacation, then end up using it for a down payment on investment property. But since mortgage lenders don't like to see borrowed down payments, these investors often restrict themselves to properties where the mortgages can be assumed, few questions asked, or where VTB financing is available.

But once you have real estate experience and substantial assets, institutional lenders are more willing to advance you mortgage monies when the down payment is borrowed.

An important thing to remember about many of these creative

techniques is that usually you can only use them in inverse proportion to the general level of real estate activity in your area.

In a seller's market, virtually none of these techniques will be usable. Then all most sellers understand — and are comfortable with — is a "cash" sale. Even vendor-take-backs turn them off. But as the market shifts to a balanced situation, and they're obliged to listen to reason, you can use more and more of these creative techniques. In a buyer's market, let your creativity run free.

CHAPTER 9

Mortgage Brokers

Just as real estate brokers bring together buyers and sellers, mortgage brokers bring together borrowers seeking funds and lenders seeking mortgages. Mortgage brokers ordinarily don't have funds of their own; they act as intermediaries.

Mortgage brokers are licensed to arrange mortgage financing with mortgage lenders. Mortgage lenders may be private individuals or groups, or public institutions, particularly trust, loan and savings companies. Banks, credit unions, life insurers and caisses populaires tend to deal directly with borrowers. Occasionally, brokers make mortgage loans on their own account, though these are almost always resold.

Depending on the province, mortgage brokers are a separately licensed trade or may also be mortgage brokers by virtue of being real estate brokers or may not be licensed at all. Lawyers often act as mortgage brokers, too.

At one time, mortgage brokers played a larger part in real estate transactions than they do now. But ever since trust companies were first allowed to do mortgage lending in 1967, mortgage brokers have played a decreasing part in arranging first mortgages for the average homeowner and small investor.

Today, their major role has shifted to:

• placing difficult and marginal mortgages, particularly high-ratio insured ones
• arranging secondary mortgage financing
• channeling private funds into the mortgage market
• acting as intermediaries for the purchase and sale of vendor-take-back mortgages
• expanding the mortgage origination capability of small mortgage lending institutions.

If you're an average home buyer or small investor, your first choice for financing — after the seller — is usually your corner financial institution. Going that route saves you the mortgage broker's fees and the rates and terms are usually better. One mortgage broker told me about the easiest money he ever made. A homeowner approached him, seeking second-mortgage money. The broker simply asked the first-mortgage lender if it would advance a second and it agreed.

Sometimes, though, a mortgage broker can be invaluable.

Take the case where the borrower had a home worth about $120,000 with a $60,000 vendor-take-back mortgage coming due. He was unemployed, but had $40,000 cash with which he was planning to open a small business. The banks turned him down flat. But a mortgage broker was able to arrange financing with an "equity lender" so he could pay off the vendor-take-back loan. An equity lender is simply an institution that is more concerned with the value of the property than the borrower's ability to make the mortgage payments.

In another instance, the borrower was trying to get a CMHC high ratio loan, but the monthly carrying costs were $50 above his limit. But by knowing exactly how CMHC calculated these costs, the broker was able to suggest a way for the buyer to meet the requirement.

Knowledgeable mortgage brokers are invaluable to buyers whose GDS and TDS ratios are right at the edge. As mentioned earlier, the 30% GDS ratio is merely a general guideline; some institutions push it up a few percentage points, others reduce it. The exact ratio varies, depending on the particular institution's underwriting experience, its supply of funds and its attitude towards risk in general. Good mortgage brokers know which institutions and investors are willing to accept the marginal risks.

Where the institution has had a good record of referrals from a mortgage broker, it may greatly ease its requirements on a deal. Some brokers claim their default record with some institutions is better than mortgages originated by the institution directly.

It's important that you deal with experienced brokers — licensed where required — with a history of standing behind their commitments. Ethical real estate brokers know who they are and have an interest in working with them. After all, if the "commitment" you get turns out to be worthless and there's no financing, there'll be no deal and no commission. And certainly no repeat business from you.

Difficult times, especially, seem to bring out mortgage scam artists seeking to capitalize on the plight of desperate homeowners, small businesspeople and in-over-their-heads investors. You've seen the enticing newspaper ads offering mortgage money regardless of your credit. Some of these offers are from legitimate brokers. But many are come-ons from unlicensed larcenists whose only aim is a non-refundable, often illegal, application fee. Ontario law, for instance, forbids a mortgage broker from accepting any deposit or advance payment for arranging a mortgage of less than $200,000.

When you're borrowing money through a mortgage broker, you're considered a "consumer" and the broker must comply with certain disclosure and other rules under your provincial mortgage broker's act and/or separate consumer protection legislation.

Before dealing with a mortgage broker, get a full statement of the rules from your local provincial consumer affairs ministry or mortgage brokers act registrar or administrator.

* * *

In dealing with private lenders and unscrupulous mortgage brokers, you should be on guard for a host of tricks that can cost you dearly and may well be illegal. Private mortgage lenders display a never-ending ingenuity in creating new charges and ways to increase their yields on mortgage loans to gullible, desperate or injudicious borrowers. They charge the mortgagor all kinds of up-front fees for application, inspection, appraisal. Then they may add in "premiums," "discounts," "dues," "subscriptions" and "disbursements." They may also provide for improper discharge fees, if they can get away with it. This latter fee violates Section 8 of the federal *Interest Act*, which forbids penalties of any kind for discharging a mortgage on maturity. Lately, too, some lenders have been importing U.S. bafflegab in the form of "points" — that is, charging the borrower a percentage of the mortgage loan up-front.

The cumulative effect of all these charges can easily raise your effective annual interest rate to the triple-digit range.

Such arrangements could well violate provincial "unconscionable transactions" acts. There's no blanket rule as to what constitutes an unconscionable transaction; each case can only be decided based on its circumstances. And, of course, then only if the mortgagor/borrower takes court action.

Factors that the courts consider include:

• lack of full disclosure in language intelligible to the borrower
• the respective experience of the parties
• whether the lender was taking undue advantage of the borrower because of the borrower's urgency for the funds
• the risk involved in the loan — taking into consideration the value of the mortgaged property, the borrower's ability to repay the loan and his credit rating
• the cost of the loan with relation to the prevailing market in the area for the same general type of loan involving a similar risk
• whether the documentation securing the loan is fair and reasonable

under the circumstances or whether it contains provisions that might cause the borrower serious problems while not being necessary to protect the lender.[29]

If you suspect you've been victimized in an unconscionable transaction, call your provincial consumer relations ministry or have a chat with your lawyer. It could be a worthwhile investment.

CHAPTER 10

Lawyers

Lawyers are an essential element in most real estate transactions. But as with every other tradesman you employ, their expertise is limited, their self-interest sometimes unlimited. Some investors "burned" by their lawyers would say they have more tricks up their sleeves than unscrupulous mechanics working on a stranded motorist's car.

Across Canada, several dozens of lawyers are disbarred, reprimanded, suspended, or otherwise disciplined every year. Others are jailed for theft — like the Upper Canada College graduate who defrauded the trust company he owned, as well as another trust company and business associates, of at least $1.5 million. One lawyer even achieved a spot on the RCMP's most-wanted list — he disappeared with more than $2-million of his clients' funds.

Of course, lawyers face great temptations. Funds from buyers, banks and mortgagors are paid into their trust accounts as a matter of course. By contrast, real estate companies usually only hold the purchaser's deposits and these rarely exceed the commissions that the agents are due.

Lawyers are expert — at least, they're presumed to be — in the legal aspects of real estate. They can search the record of ownership of the property to be sure you have a good title. They should be able to advise you as to zoning and restrictions on the property and how the rezoning process works. They should be able to draw up the property documents for passing title, for leasing property, creating options, selling property and for building and architectural contracts.

What they are not expert in is real estate investment. Of course, lawyers invest in real estate; some are even successful. But many of the worst real estate investments you could imagine have been purchased by lawyers.

"Do we listen to what our lawyers say? Of course not," says Rafael Ghermezian, one of the brothers who created the multi-billion dollar

West Edmonton Mall. "They do what we tell them. If they don't, we hire someone else."

Still, some lawyers are free with their advice regarding what price you should sell or buy a property for. Overwhelmingly, it's advice worth disregarding.

For example, in a recent estate settlement, the lawyer recommended a listing price of $89,000. The first day of the listing, twelve offers were registered and the home sold for $98,000. The buyer did some minor repairs and resold it a month later for $118,000. When curious real estate agents asked the lawyer why he had suggested such an obviously low listing price, he said he wanted a "quick sale" and didn't want to "waste his time" on it. So, for the lawyer's convenience, the heirs lost a potential $18,000.

Uninformed advice can work the other way too. In another case, the lawyer recommended against a sale at a certain price. He hadn't seen the house or other real estate sales figures. But, he said, he used to live in the city 20 years ago and he just "thought it should sell for more." Fortunately, the heirs went against their lawyer's advice and sold the house — bordering a junkyard.

Lawyer's services are just like any other consumer commodity. And the same rules of *caveat emptor* that govern the rest of the market apply equally to lawyers. Perhaps more so. Expertise, ethics and fees vary widely. While hiring a lawyer is essential for your protection, it's just as important to protect yourself *from* your lawyer.

If you weren't told differently, a couple years of dealing with real estate lawyers would lead you to conclude that cupidity and negligence were the professional norm. You can't go wrong taking that view and acting accordingly.

To begin with, discuss fully and frankly what the lawyer will be charging you. Don't let it be an unpleasant surprise. If it's a complicated deal, he may charge you a small fee for this consultation, $50 to $100. There are no standard fees; and federal law prohibits fixed rates.

However, the Canadian Bar Association's Guide to Legal Fees suggests lawyers bill $70 to $175 an hour on real estate transactions. In Ontario, the Association suggests that the average house purchase requires eight to twelve hours of solicitor's time plus six to seven hours of para-legal fees; in addition, the buyer is responsible for other charges such as realty taxes, estoppel certificates and so forth.

Acting for the seller in a typical Ontario house sale takes three to four hours of the lawyer's time and a further two to four hours of para-legal time, says the Association.

In practice, these generous guidelines serve the same function as the guidebooks so beloved by certain auto garages. For handling the same house purchase transaction, different lawyers will charge you anywhere from $450 to $1,600 and more. Newer, just-licenced lawyers will be eager to offer low rates and are usually no less competent than their higher-priced colleagues.

Price alone, though, shouldn't be your sole guide. If a lawyer quotes an extraordinarily low fee, he may be skimping on his effort, shuffling all the work onto unsupervised employees or even not searching title at all, figuring the work was done properly by some other lawyer along the line. And even if the fee is reasonable, he or she may tack on a host of "disbursements" at the end to more than make up for it.

In discussing fees, beware that verbal quotes from lawyers are frequently worth the paper they're printed on. Take the lawyer who recently quoted a $600 inclusive charge for handling the sale of a property. But when he deducted his fees from the mortgage proceeds he added in $350 for preparing the mortgage. When the client questioned the charge, he attributed the $350 to a "misunderstanding" — naturally, the client's.

Interestingly, the same lawyer certified to the buyer, and to the lender who advanced a $96,000 mortgage, that the purchaser had "a good and marketable title to the premises" — despite the fact that the only survey he had of the property was done before the house was built!

To protect yourself from misunderstandings over fees, it's a good idea to discuss them frankly with your lawyer. Then send him or her a confirming letter, by registered mail, detailing that understanding.

You should exercise great caution when it comes to written directions regarding the disbursement of funds. Most disbarments stem from lawyers stealing mortgage funds — either funds they are "investing" or that they are supposed to be using to discharge mortgage loans you owe.

Say you are selling a property and have agreed to discharge a mortgage. The lawyer usually asks you to sign a direction making all funds payable to himself because 1) it's more convenient for him; and 2) this arrangement thus insures that he is paid his fee and costs; he simply deducts it from the proceeds. However, you can insist that the funds coming from the purchaser or his lender be made directly payable to you or to your mortgagee, not the lawyer. If he wishes to ensure receiving his fee, you can make a direction for that amount to him.

Be extremely careful when you're paying off a private mortgage. In such a situation, it's common for the lawyer to ask for the funds to be paid to him in trust. But you should do so only on a written direction from the mortgagee. Furthermore, you should not hand the lawyer the cheque until you see a discharge signed by the mortgagee. No discharge, no cheque.

Unfortunately, in most private mortgages where a lawyer is involved, you'll be hit with a $100 to $200 fee for "preparing" the discharge; i.e., filling in several blanks on a standard form. Small trust and loan companies, too, are fond of this revenue-producing scam. Interestingly, the large banks often don't levy discharge fees.

Can you save money by using the same lawyer as the other party to the transaction?

You can. And it's not illegal for a lawyer to do this. But the Bar Associations strongly urge their members not to do so because of the inherent conflict of interest. A lawyer is not an impartial referee; he or she should represent your best interests in a transaction.

CHAPTER 11

Overall Strategies

All roads may lead to Rome. But not all roads lead to real estate riches. Not all strategies for acquiring and profiting from real estate investment work all the time everywhere. What's suited for one city, even one block within that city, may be next to useless in another city, another block. Your number-one strategy in Toronto may well be number 59 in Montreal.

As well, real estate investment is *cyclical*. What works well in one part of the cycle will separate you from your shirt (or blouse) in the next.

How you behave as a real estate investor is largely based on your individual investment orientation. It will determine the kind of property you buy, how much you're willing to pay for it, the risk you're willing to assume, the work you're willing to do and the time you can wait for gains.

Fortunately, real estate affords opportunities for all types of investors — from conservative investors oriented to long-term capital gains and steadily increasing income, to twitchy speculative types who can't stand still. And all shades of personalities in between.

There's no reason though why you can't sample investments from every part of the spectrum. Choose short-term investments for a quick turnover and no management responsibilities. Look to longer-term investments for yearly cash flow and tax benefits on resale.

Overall factors you should always keep in mind include:

Location
The oldest saying in real estate investment says that the three most important things in real estate are "location, location, location." While there's still truth in the saying, there are practical difficulties in applying it. Separated from the criteria of price and management, location alone isn't enough to base an investment decision on.

First, even when the admonition is known, many investors have strange notions of just what constitutes a good location and what doesn't. I'll never forget listening to one investor enthusiastically describe his home's excellent location, while gazing out over the adjacent 50 acres of rail switching yards.

Secondly, the premium price demanded by an "excellent" location may render it a less profitable investment than a property in an "infirm" location. So if, for example, the homes with the Casey Jones view were purchased for a low enough price, there may actually be more profit on reselling them than in buying swank homes in the trendiest part of town. In other words, always relate "inferior"/"superior" location with potential profitability.

Thirdly, location is often "good" or "bad" only in relation to a specific use. Thus a downtown 100-year-old multi-level building may be a poor location for a manufacturer, but it could be perfect for professional offices and trendy retailing.

Don't Get Hung Up on Losses

Sure, it's great to make money on every property you buy. But it's no disgrace if you don't. If a property is a loser, or it's causing you too much emotional grief, drop it. Another and better opportunity will come along.

Losses are only a disgrace in business if you don't learn something from them. Pick up any issue of *Business Week* and you'll read how some multi-millionaire entrepreneur or successful company at one time or another wrote off losses of millions, even hundreds of millions of dollars.

Even experienced real estate investors make mistakes. One well-known investment guru passed up a number of investment properties because the owners demanded one or two thousand dollars above his self-imposed spending limits. In each case, another investor bought the properties and within a year "mortgaged" out of them — that is, took out mortgage loans equivalent to his down payment. And he still continued to receive a substantial return in the form of rents.

Don't Wait for the Perfect Property

One investor professed to be eager to participate in the market. Yet every time she looked at a property she could find nothing but flaws and risks. North of Dundas Street? Why that's too close to the tracks. Three stories and five bedrooms? Too big. The kitchen has to be rearranged: where will I put the stove?

Of course, missing opportunities can't be avoided. Indeed, most lives are a series of missed opportunities. But if you're waiting for complete safety from risk and invulnerability to ineptitude, you're waiting in vain. Death and taxes are your only guarantees.

60

Don't Be Impatient

Like getting advice from your parents (or giving it to your children), this suggestion is easier said than done.

Witness an investor who bought four downtown houses a few years ago. Real estate values remained stagnant for several years. So he surrendered to impatience and sold three of the houses. On one he lost $3,000, on another $4,000 and on the third made $15,000. But thanks to a procrastinating contractor doing repair work on the final house, he delayed selling it till the following year. On that one, he made $40,000. And if he had held the other properties another year, he would have seen a further $154,000. Impatience can carry a high price tag.

Don't Get Emotionally Involved with Your Property

Many texts on real estate investment mention a benefit called "pride of ownership." Well, it certainly doesn't hurt to take pride in your property's appearance. After all, it may get you a better rent and a higher price on resale. But if "pride" is all you're getting out of your investment, it's time for another investment.

Conservative Assumptions of Inflation

One well-known real estate lecturer blithely tells his $600-a-day students how they can become "millionaires in eight years by buying four $75,000 properties every year" with only 10% down. By the end of ten years, he says you'll have accumulated 32 properties and have a net worth of $1 million. The secret behind this growth is an assumption of 10% annual inflation in real estate values. Take a few minutes and you can draw yourself an even more impressive scenario for free — just assume an inflation rate of 20%.

Certainly, well-chosen real estate will increase in value over time. But basing your investment strategy on continued high rates of increase for real estate will only lead to disappointment and foolish investment decisions.

Avoid the Herd Instinct

This is the instinct that lines people up to buy gold at $800 an ounce; or camping out overnight for a chance to spend money. When others are lining up to buy is the time to sell. Conversely, when buyers are scarce is exactly the time to buy.

Never Underestimate the Value of Opportunism

Just because you're planning or searching for one type of investment is no reason not to go in a completely different direction if the occasion arises. The successful pursuit of profit demands economic flexibility. An institution can't deviate instantly from set goals. But you, the individual entrepreneur, can. Once you're thoroughly grounded in the mechanics of real estate investment, serendipity can work wonders. In other words, opportunities come to those who are prepared, and those who are prepared exploit the opportunities when they come.

CHAPTER 12

Figuring Out What Price to Pay

The other side of measuring return is figuring out what to pay for a specific property.

Of course, the lowest price possible! But what's low? What's high? What's appropriate? For the successful small investor, the decision always combines:

1. Traditional appraisal techniques.
2. A careful evaluation of future possibilities.
3. Shrewd and careful bargaining strategies and tactics.

The Traditional Appraisal

As explained in chapter 13, appraisers rely on three basic approaches in determining market value — comparative market data, cost and income. But essential as the appraisal industry might be — and fascinating as it might be — the individual investor who puts much faith in any appraiser's conclusions is riding for a fall. Still, the three approaches they use are valuable, as long as you're aware of their limitations.

Comparative Market Data — The comparative market data approach is easily understandable. Therefore people — including the courts — tend to put a lot of reliance on it. Certainly in the hands of a skilled appraiser — licensed or not — it is a good method of broadly determining what's a reasonable price to pay (or get) for property. In any community, there are likely to have been a number of recent sales of similar single-family homes, duplexes, store/apartment combinations.

But the comparative market data approach falls down when it comes to very large properties because there simply are no comparables. Try finding comparables for the West Edmonton Mall, the CN Tower, B.C. Place or Olympic Stadium!

And even when it comes to small properties, the comparative approach has several inescapable drawbacks:

- many of the characteristics of the sale are unavailable, unrevealed, and unquantifiable
- each piece of real estate is unique.
- comparables are always in the past.

Unless you've made a close physical inspection of so-called comparables, you can never be sure that they truly are comparable. Lovemaking isn't the only thing that goes on behind closed doors. Beautiful improvements and hideous house abuse are equally hidden by a bland facade.

Furthermore, the appraiser doesn't know the individual motivations that are as much part of the sale as the physical property.

The vendor, for instance, may have been dying. So extracting the maximum dollar from his property for his heirs may have been his least concern. Or the buyer may have been particularly attracted by a feature that would not have attracted the "average" buyer. Equally likely, he may not have been aware of some drawback that kept more careful buyers away. Several years ago, an eager house-hunter fell in love with a renovated three-family home at an exceptional price. So, after one nighttime visit to an unfamiliar downtown neighborhood she bought the property. On moving in, she found the bargain price had something to do with the discreetly concealed but odoriferous abattoir across the street.

Tax considerations have a tremendous impact, too. The special treatment of capital gains and principal residences affect property values. Continuing tax reform will bring further changes. The 1986 tax reform in the United States has rendered "the sales comparison approach obsolete in the near term for investment properties," concludes one consultant there.[30]

As well, the market is always changing. Just because a property fetched "x" dollars yesterday — let alone last week or last month or three months ago — is absolutely no reason to assume that it's "worth" that today. It may be worth much more. Or much less. Economic factors are ever-changing.

This isn't just an academic quibble. Take the case of a homeowner selling his home at the start of the 1981 real estate boom. To save paying a real estate commission, he decided to sell privately, basing his asking price on an appraisal from a professionally qualified appraiser. After studying the relevant comparables, the appraiser concluded the home was worth $67,000. When the first buyer appeared, the vendor showed him the appraisal and the buyer readily paid the suggested price. Meanwhile, the homeowner next door listed his inferior property with an agent for $91,900, and promptly sold it for $91,000 the first day the listing appeared.

Was the appraiser incompetent? Did the vendor have a cause of action against him? Possibly so. But the appraiser simply went by the book: he used market comparables that were, in fact, incomparable. He was out of touch with a soaring market.

Interestingly, the buyer of the $91,000 home was also relying on market comparables. But by the time of closing three months later, the market had collapsed and he would have been lucky to have resold the house for $75,000.

Appraisers couldn't keep up with changes in the recently completed boom 'n' bust ride either. The best they could often do was "adjust" 1% to 5% up or down a month.

If counting too much on out-of-date market comparables can leave you with a poor investment, it can also blind you to opportunities. Consider the case of the couple who offered to buy a small rental property for $67,000. Their offer was conditional on obtaining financing. However, the trust company they approached for funds appraised the property as worth only $60,000. So they dropped the idea. Two months later the property sold for $63,500. And three years after that it sold for $126,000.

The lesson is: *Market comparables don't necessarily have any relation to the future direction of prices.*

The Cost Approach — This is the least useful approach to value. In reality, property buyers constantly pay much more and much less than the value indicated by this approach.

A building, for instance, may be wonderfully built but an entirely inappropriate use of the land. So the building's market value is less than zero. A buyer will have to pay to demolish and remove it.

On the other hand, a building with, say, a favorable long-term lease in place with a "Triple A" tenant will be much more valuable than the same building standing empty. A long-term lease signed by a chartered bank or a government liquor store, for instance, ensures you'll receive the agreed-on stream of rental payments. In that case, the cost of reproducing the building is certainly interesting but hardly definitive; the leases have greatly influenced the property's value.

Income Capitalization Techniques — The most frequently cited problem with this approach is selecting the capitalization rate to use.

Some appraisal texts say the capitalization rate is a rate that combines the return on a safe investment such as government savings bonds, plus some premium; others say simply it is the rate a "prudent" investor is willing to accept.

However, these theories are hard put to explain the behavior of investors who in some markets regularly buy investment properties with cap rates below the inflation rate. Or even with negative cap rates.

So rather than delve into what the cap rate "should be," many investors use the cap rate as a way of tracking what other people are willing to pay for properties. So if, for instance, the current cap rate for apartment buildings ranges from 6% to 8%, then the smart investor looks to buy a property with a cap rate of at least 9%.

Even when you have a cap rate in mind, it's hard to accurately predict what your income and expenses will be on the property. A slight error gets Magnified when you capitalize it. In other words, you may think you're buying a property at a 9% cap rate, but you may actually be buying it at 7%, or 5% or less. When you buy an investment property, expenses are inevitably higher than you project, and revenues inevitably lower.

From the active investor's point of view, the problem with all these approaches is that they leave as little room for imagination as that displayed by the institutional bureaucrats they're designed to satisfy.

Evaluating Future Possibilities
The most successful investors are future-oriented. While they don't ignore the lessons of the past, their major interest is in what change is coming and where.

So, for instance, buying investment property with a "low" return may defy the income capitalization approach. But the investor may have a better perception of future property values and income potential than other investors.

Here are three elements of the future that will inevitably affect every individual property:

1. Local physical changes and developments: Such things as improved or changing transportation, new highways, rapid transit, parks and nearby real estate developments. For instance, as soon as it was announced that a century-old heavy machinery factory in a downtown area was to become a high-tech center, neighborhood housing values shot up.

2. The overall economic health of the country and the community: You can't do anything to affect these trends, but you should track them. And try to anticipate them. For example, while Calgary and Edmonton remained in the economic doldrums in 1986, some of the wealthiest Canadian families were quietly acquiring major companies and real estate there at bargain prices. Similarly, while Ontario was suffering through the worst recession since the Dirty Thirties, Asian and other investors were feeding on the breakup of Toronto-based real estate giants.

3. Untapped potential in the property itself: Here's where the small investor has the most control. You can't raise regional economic health singlehandedly. But you can raise a second floor on a house you own. You can raise rents. You can seek rezoning, severance and redevelopment.

For every property you look at, ask: Will physical changes add value? To what extent will better management improve cash flow? And, specifically, how can that cash flow be improved, maintained and capitalized on?

Shrewd Bargaining

Astute negotiating is worth every bit as much as the painstaking analyses preceding the investment decision.

Boasts one successful investor: "I make money no matter what kind of market we're in. I always buy below the market." Sometimes he buys at the asking price with large VTB financing; other times, he makes an all-cash offer for well below the asking price. Attitude plays a large part, too. His approach is always "take it or leave it." But pleasantly. "Sure, I'd *love* to give you your asking price. But it's just not warranted. I've got partners. How can I explain it to them?"

And having faith in your own decisions doesn't hurt.

To take an example: Two investors, each with the same amount of capital, concentrated on acquiring properties in a neighborhood they concluded would appreciate in the following few years. One looked at dozens of properties, made a half-dozen offers and eventually bought two properties using very little leverage. The high prices "just didn't make sense," he said. They just had to come down. The other investor, using every bit of leverage he could muster, bought two dozen properties. Admittedly, his indiscriminate shopping spree left him with some "dogs" — poorly built to begin with and run-down over the years. But all the properties were in the targeted neighborhood.

Both investors chose the right neighborhood for the right reasons. But the second, showing more confidence in his own judgment, reaped 20 times the return of the first.

Paying close attention to the ever-changing market cannot be over-emphasized.

CHAPTER 13

Real Estate Appraisers

Real estate appraisers and the appraisals they do are a vital part of every real estate transaction. Knowing how they arrive at their valuations of real property can benefit you as an investor, both when you're seeking financing and when you're buying or selling property.

Appraisals are needed for:

* settling estates and divorces
* partnership dissolutions
* corporate financial statements
* assuring lenders that they're not "over mortgaging" — that is, lending a higher percentage of a property's value than the mortgage is supposed to represent
* justifying institutional property acquisitions to shareholders and government regulators
* establishing property taxes
* verifying damage claims resulting from fire, wind, rain, hail and other natural disasters
* determining just compensation for property being taken for government use
* challenging excessive tax assessments, capital gain payments and other taxes
* supporting damage claims in court actions.

Appraisers usually define *market value* as "the highest price in terms of money which the property will bring to a willing seller if exposed for sale on the open market allowing a reasonable time to find a willing purchaser, buying with the knowledge of all the uses to which it is adapted and for which it is legally capable of being used, and with neither party acting under necessity, compulsion or peculiar and special circumstances."[31]

68

Traditionally, appraisers have relied on three approaches to determining market value. And when they have determined the value of the property by each of these methods, they "reconcile" them to arrive at a final market value.[32]

Comparative Market Analysis — Also called the *direct sales comparison* method, this technique requires the appraiser to find properties similar to the subject property that have been recently sold, or offered for sale. The more similar the property is — and the closer in time when it was sold to the date of the appraisal — the better is the comparison.

The appraiser tries to adjust for any differences in time of the sale, location and physical characteristics between the subject property and the comparable property. If he's appraising an income property, adjustments may also be made for differences in income. Differing financing characteristics can also be taken into account, e.g., an all-cash deal vs. one that is highly levered.

The appraiser also adjusts the value of the comparables he's analyzing in relation to the subject property — down if it's better than the subject property, up if it's inferior.

Say you're an appraiser and the property you're asked to evaluate isn't quite as big, for example, as a comparable property. You adjust for this difference by deducting some amount from the price that the *comparable* actually sold for. (You might base it on a square foot basis or the number of rooms). Conversely, if the comparable property is inferior in some way to the subject property, you raise the value of the comparable.

In other words, if the property you're analyzing has additional features that the market puts a value on, you raise the price of the comparable. If it doesn't have the positive features of the comparable, and maybe even has some negatives, you lower the price of the comparable.

Reproduction Cost — In this approach, also called the *summation* approach, the appraiser determines the cost of reproducing (rebuilding) any existing structures on the land, then deducts any depreciation and obsolescence. Lastly, the depreciated cost is added to the value of the land as if it were vacant. If the building is on leased land, the appraiser has to determine the value of the leasehold interest.

Income Capitalization — This is the most complex way of determining market value and the one most often applied in valuing income-earning real estate. It's regarded as the most accurate as it *most closely approximates the way investors approach valuing properties*. However, it is of virtually no use in smaller properties. You should have at least five to ten units in an apartment building or several commercial units before giving much weight to capitalization methods.

There are a number of ways of capitalizing income.

The most common method is called *net income capitalization* — also known as *overall* or *composite* capitalization. The appraiser first determines the probable income stream from the property on a "free and clear" basis — that is, as if there were no debt on the property. Then he divides the indicated *net income* figure by the capitalization rate or "cap rate" that he deems appropriate; this rate is usually determined by the cap rate of sales of similar properties.

To illustrate: Assume you're buying a $350,000 ten-plex that has an annual projected net income of $38,000. The general formula is:

$$\frac{\text{Income}}{\text{Sale Price}} = \text{Capitalization rate}$$

So: $\dfrac{\$38,000}{\$350,000} = .10857$ or 10.85

As long as you know any two elements in the equation, you can calculate the third.

What if the same property has a projected net income of $38,000 but there is no asking price? Simply divide the net income by the cap rate:

So: $\dfrac{I}{R} = V$ Or: $\dfrac{\$38,000}{10.85\%} = \$350,230$

Say you know the price and the cap rate: Then it's $V \times R = I$

So: $\$350,000 \times 10.85\% = \$38,000$

A more sophisticated capitalization approach that is frequently used seeks to separate the yield attributable to the debt from the yield on the equity. The aim of these *mortgage-equity techniques* is to derive an overall capitalization rate based on these different expectations. For example, say the mortgage rate is 11%, the property is financed 75% and the investor is assumed to want a return on his 25% equity of 6%, the then current rate on bank savings accounts.

Mortgage 11% x 75 = 8.25%
Equity   6% x 25 = 1.5%
Total   9.75% overall capitalization rate

The appraiser then applies the overall rate to the building's income to derive a value for the property. So, in the above example, if you applied the 9.75% to an apartment building yielding $100,000 in annual net income, you would come up with a value of $1,025,641 by using the capitalization formula:

$$\frac{\text{Income}}{\text{Rate}} = \text{Value} \quad \text{Or:} \quad \frac{\$100,000}{9.75\%} = \$1,025.641$$

More sophisticated income capitalization techniques attempt to account for changes in annual operating income, the time-value of money, recapture of depreciation and different terminal values of the property, as when you sell it. These methods are rarely applied to properties costing less than several million dollars.

After applying one or more of these methods to the property in question, the appraiser "reconciles" all the values into a final "estimate of value." Reconciliation involves giving the most weight to the most reliable data and to the method that is most appropriate for the type of property being appraised.

As an investor, usually you won't be retaining an appraiser directly. Rather, the lender you're dealing with will appoint its own appraiser and then simply charge you for the report. If you're obtaining an appraisal yourself for other purposes, keep in mind that there are several levels of appraisal.

It may be sufficient to have a real estate broker give you an impartial written "opinion of value." This is not, by the way, the same thing as asking a salesperson or broker to give you his idea of what your property is worth so you can list it with him for sale.

More expensive and more detailed appraisals are also available from members of the Appraisal Institute of Canada, the national professional society of real estate appraisers founded in 1938. Institute members have two designations: CRA (Canadian Residential Appraiser) for individuals qualified in the appraisal and valuation of individual undeveloped residential building sites and dwellings with not more than three self-contained family housing units; and AACI (Accredited Appraiser Canadian Institute) for appraisal of just about anything. Appraisers also provide feasibility and consulting services, which are essential if you're proposing a large project to a lender.

The Ontario Real Estate Association, Ontario Real Estate Boards and the Canadian Real Estate Association are also promoting accredited Market Value Appraisers — Residential (MVA). Although its sponsors say the MVA program meets or exceeds all requirements established by CMHC, institutional lenders generally scoff at MVAs. Mainly, they're miffed that they weren't consulted when the program was instituted. Lenders also have their prejudices about particular AACIs in their community. So before you engage any appraisers be sure their work will be accepted by whomever is requiring it.

CHAPTER 14

Inspecting a Property

Home Inspectors

The idea behind home inspection is certainly sensible. After all, you probably wouldn't buy a $3,000 or $4,000 used car without getting a mechanic to check it over. Yet every day people buy $250,000 homes because they like the decor and landscaping.

Over the past several years, there has been a tremendous growth in the home inspection business. For a fee of typically between $250 to $400, inspectors check over property on which a buyer has put or is thinking of putting an offer on. Inspectors note the details of construction, and faults in major and minor components of the property — everything from the need to paint downspouts to structural defects.

Unfortunately, the concept of home inspection can break down in practice. Inspection reports vary in accuracy. And even when they are accurate, you should not let them deter you from the more important aspects of the investment opportunity.

There are no legal standards for home inspection, no government involvement in setting standards or licensing. Anyone with a clipboard, a convincing name and a ready opinion can call himself a home inspector. In fact, many do. However, in 1989, a voluntary organization was created in Ontario — the now 40-member Ontario Association of Home Inspectors — which operates as a chapter of the non-profit American Society of Home Inspectors. There are also chapters in British Columbia, Quebec, the Prairie provinces and Ottawa. The group subscribes to a code of ethics and a set of inspection standards. These outline the housing components and systems that an inspector should observe and describe, and those he is not required to observe.

Some inspection firms use people with architectural or engineering degrees, which are impressive to the uninitiated. But without practical experience in renovating homes, their expertise is suspect.

Whatever their training or background, rarely does one person have sufficient expertise to thoroughly inspect all the systems in a home. Heating, plumbing and wiring can be a minor mystery to them. Experience is the key. And while architects may sometimes have that, so do renovation contractors, builders and tradesmen.

Instead of hiring a general home inspector, you might be better served having the individual components you're most concerned about inspected by specialists. If your major concern is the roof — because you see signs of water damage — have a roofer look at it. If you're worried about water problems in the basement, call in a waterproofing firm. If you're bothered by a crack in the basement wall, call in an experienced renovation contractor, architect or structural engineer to check it out. If there's a septic system, call in a septic specialist.

If termites are present in your area — as they are in southern Ontario and British Columbia — you might want termite specialists to check the property. Even if they discover these wood-eating pests, you don't have to abandon the property. Termites can be controlled through chemical treatments and physical barrier.

Inspectors tend to offer two types of inspection — a quick verbal (or written) one or a detailed written evaluation. The longer ones are more expensive. But do you really need several pages noting the condition of each window in the house? the location of the doors and their condition? the number of electrical outlets? the number of closets and the like? If you can't figure out these things for yourself or can't be bothered to, perhaps you shouldn't be directly investing in real estate anyway.

What you do want is some outside opinion on is the condition of the basic structure, as well as the major components of the property.[33] However, some problems are so obvious you usually don't need an expert to spot them. Just open your own eyes. These include:

- *Basement flooding and severe dampness* — High-water marks on the walls, excessive mustiness, recent repairs and water on the floor are sure signs of problems.
- *Structural and ground support flaws*, which are revealed in uneven settlement and large cracks in walls and foundations.
- *Insulation* — The biggest concern is the presence of urea formaldehyde foam insulation (UFFY). Where possible, your offer should have a clause whereby the vendor warrants that the property has never been insulated with UFFI. But in many instances this isn't possible — as in estate sales, or where the lender is selling the property because the borrower has defaulted on his mortgage obligations, or in sales by the public trustee when property owners die without a will or heirs.
  If the property is brick, you can often spot a UFFI installation

by a telltale series of patched holes in the exterior walls. But sometimes UFFI was placed only in one or two interior walls, or only in a portion of an outside wall. Other signs to look for are smooth new interior walls and new siding. Removing switch plates and electrical outlet covers may reveal the foam. If it's light yellow with an irregular bubbly surface it's likely to be UFFI. But be careful not to confuse UFFI with safe polymeric foam sealants used to seal air leaks around door frames, sill plates, etc.

- *Termites* are another hidden problem frequently found in southern Ontario and British Columbia.[34] Many uninformed homeowners don't realize they have a termite problem until a door mysteriously falls off its hinges or the floor under the bathtub starts sagging. Or the book under their bed is devoured by hungry termites.

  Because termites hate light, they burrow through the wood and feed on it from the inside out till you have only a veneer over a honeycombed interior. To get to the wood while avoiding light they build "shelter tubes" of compacted soil. These show up on fences, foundation walls, planting ties, retaining walls and structural members of the house and are a sure sign of termites. Pay special attention to damp areas of the basement near laundry tubs and drains. But sometimes there are no ready signs. Hollow concrete block foundation walls, for instance, provide perfect concealed entryways; the termites come up through the center of the blocks, so they don't leave their telltale tubes.

  Carpenter ants are another common insect pest. Though beneficial in the wild and as insect predators, they have a voracious appetite for cellulose destruction. Unlike termites, they don't eat the wood they tunnel through. So they leave visible trails of sawdust. Carpenter ants like nesting in hollow panelled doors, under washing machines, dishwashers and other damp areas, behind baseboards and fireplaces and in basements and attics.

- *"Improvements" and alterations by previous owners* are often more of a problem than original defects. Several years ago, a naive investor bought a home with an income apartment in the basement. But when he set about further renovations, he found that the foundation walls had been totally undermined and a number of first-floor joists severed to create headroom. Untreated, the house was in danger of collapsing — along with the neighboring house it was attached to. A quick expenditure of $10,000 kept the house upright, but cut deeply into the investor's expectations of profit.

Of course, you should also check out the roof and the heating, plumbing and electrical systems. But faults and deficiencies in these areas are rarely fatal. You can usually closely estimate the costs of putting them in order and work those calculations into your purchase negotiations.

Besides these purely mechanical considerations, you should keep in mind ways that you can economically upgrade the property. What is its income potential? How can you rearrange the space to derive more rental units? higher rents? different uses?

CHAPTER 15

Profiting from an Agent

Choosing the Right Agent

Selling real estate is perceived by many people as a glamorous career. Real estate agents dress well, smile a lot and drive big cars. If you're an agent, you simply escort buyers through beautiful, expensive homes and reap big commissions when they sign on the dotted line. What the public doesn't generally know is that 50% of newcomers to real estate sales quit in their first year and another 25% leave in the next six months. Literally thousands of people pass licensing exams every year and never sell anything.

For those who do remain, the rewards are less than impressive. According to the Canadian Real Estate Association, a full-time agent who has been in the business one or two years earns an average of only $18,000 a year. The "super" agents with six-figure annual incomes, occasionally profiled in newspapers, are extraordinary exceptions.

Even among the survivors actually making a living selling real estate, there's a world of difference in the knowledge, experience, judgment and ethical standards they bring to their trade. A good one can save you time and money; a poor one can cost you a bundle and sour you on mankind.

So how do you separate the winners from the losers? And how can you make the most of their skills?

As a general rule, choosing the right agent is more important if you're selling property than if you're buying it. As a buyer, you can switch agents if you're not satisfied with what you're being shown. But as a seller you're usually stuck for the duration of the listing.

Recommendations from friends and neighbors will probably be your first source. Successful agents, in fact, do up to 95% of their business with repeat or referral customers. You could also look for a broker who's active in the area you're buying or selling in. Who has signs on neighborhood properties? Especially "sold" signs? Sometimes the name of the salesperson who listed the property is on the sign.

But keep in mind that the company whose "sold" sign is on the property is not necessarily the one that came up with the buyer. Usually, it's simply the company that obtained the listing; another firm may well have come up with the buyer. That's because, under a multiple listing service, any real estate firm in the system can sell the property. And only in a few areas of the country is the sign of the listing company replaced with that of the selling company if they're different.

Often it helps to select a salesperson with professional qualifications beyond the salesman's license. Brokers usually have more experience and real estate education. The initials F.R.I. after a salesperson's name means that he's a Fellow of the Real Estate Institute. An F.R.I. designation usually indicates five college level courses in economics and business law and at least five years experience selling real estate. Company sales awards indicate that the agent is actually selling property.

The salesperson's approach to listing your property is a powerful guide to his professionalism. First, how does he come up with a suggested price for listing your property?

The proper way to price is on the basis of hard facts drawn from comparable market data. Without you having to ask, the agent should draw up a comparative market analysis (CMA) indicating the price you will most likely be able to obtain for your property. The CMA should show what comparable properties are on the market now and how much money their owners are asking for. These homes are your competition. The analysis should go back at least 12 months showing what similar properties have been listed for and what they have fetched. When prices are rising rapidly, the analysis doesn't have to go back that far.

Whatever the time period, ensure that the comparisons are legitimate — complete, accurate and up-to-date. For example, you don't want to compare detached houses to semi-detached houses; houses with parking to those with none; buildings with "Triple A" national tenants to those with marginal local businesses. Financing details should be included too. Were the homes sold for all cash? Or were there mortgages taken back? Perhaps even low-rate assumable mortgages? An apparently high price may be offset by good financing — a large, low-interest, vendor takeback mortgage, for instance. If VTBs are typical, you can't expect to get the same price for your property without offering the same incentive. Many real estate boards have computerized their listings and sales data so that board members have instant access to comparable sales, expiries (properties that had been listed, but had not been sold) and comparable properties currently on the market.

Marketing is important too. Putting up a sign and waiting for calls isn't enough. How is the salesperson planning to market your property? Will there be open houses? Advertising? Brochures? Listings with more than one real estate board? For large commercial listings, you should solicit formal written presentations from several brokers.

How important is the broker?

When you're choosing a brokerage firm — the company that employs the salesperson — should you look for a large company? A small one? A nationally known name? The office on the corner? An independent? Or a franchise?

The overriding trend in real estate brokerage is consolidation. The giants — both the franchise systems and the multi-office firms — have been taking increasingly larger shares of the market. In 1991, just three companies — Royal LePage Limited, Re/Max and Century 21 — with total commission income of approximately $1.255 billion accounted for more than half of residential sales.

But what does that mean for you? Surprisingly, unless you're managing a corporate move, not all that much.

There are thousands of independent brokers, ranging from one-person operations to community brokerages with up to ten offices, substantial local identity and hefty advertising budgets. The independents persist and prosper against the odds. The future doesn't necessarily belong to the biggest fish neither should your business.

Size can actually be a burden for the giant companies. The rules required in a large organization "box in and frustrate the best agents," says a successful agent who quit a large company to open his own. "To be really successful in real estate you have to be creative. In big companies you get tunnel vision and fail to see the opportunities."

Commission structure, too, plays a part in keeping the independent broker productive. To support their high overhead or franchise fees, large companies and the franchise can't pay their agents as much as the smaller ones. For instance, the basic commission split at one large brokerage firm gives the salesperson only 48% of the commission, though this can rise to 65% after the salesperson brings in a gross commission of $35,000 in a calendar year.

By contrast, independents usually pay their salespeople 60% to 75% of each commission they earn from day one. After about $25,000 in gross commission to the office, they may boost the salesperson's slice to 85% to 90% of each sale.

An increasing number of companies are adopting the commission system popularized by Re/Max. In the Re/Max-type setup, the agent or employed broker pays a flat monthly fee for office space — usually from $450 to $1200 — and keeps 95% to 100% of the commission. The point is that the salesperson with an independent or in a Re/Max-type setup, gets to keep more of each commission and therefore has greater incentive to sell your property. Of course, the large companies have many fine salespeople earning good incomes by serving their clients well. But by no means do they have a monopoly.

Different Types of Listings
A listing agreement is your contract with the broker to pay a fee for arranging the sale, lease or exchange of your property or business.

Standard form listings are prepared by legal counsel for the various real estate associations and boards. They are not government documents; and they are not reviewed by any independent body. However, they are binding on you. Basically, there are three types of listings:

Open Listings — These are listings that you, the seller, may sign with a number of brokers. The salesman who introduces the buyer to the property receives the commission and you pay nothing if you sell the property yourself. Open listings, both for sale and lease, are most common in commercial properties. Very few agents will put time and effort into a homeowner's open listing when there are other, surer, opportunities for earning a commission.

Exclusive Listings — These give one broker the right to market a property. And if the property is sold, the listing broker will be the only one able to claim a commission from the vendor. Though the listing broker may allow another broker to show the property, make an offer on it and share in the commission if it's sold, he doesn't have to. On an exclusive listing you pay a lower commission — generally 5% of the selling price versus 6% on an MLS listing, which is described below.

But there's a deadly drawback for you as the seller: instead of your property being exposed to the thousands of agents in the local MLS system, it's only exposed to buyers that the listing agent comes across. And often the listing agent with the exclusive won't cooperate with other agents. So you don't even know of the potential buyers you're missing.

"It's a selfish attitude on the part of the salespeople to push for exclusive listings," says Joseph Castaldi, a past president of the Toronto Real Estate Board. "They like exclusive listings because they get a double commission."

Exclusive listings are more common in a seller's market. Then the salesperson is likely to sell the property quickly and so is almost guaranteed a higher commission than if the property were exposed on the MLS system. For instance, the salesperson who lists and sells a $100,000 home with a 5% exclusive listing gets $4,200 (assuming a 70/30 split with his employer). But if he has to share the commission with another broker, he'll only get $2,100.

Real estate brokers specializing in plush districts sometimes push for exclusive listings on the basis that they're doing so to "protect" the seller. "We'll only show the property to 'qualified' buyers," they say. "No riff raff allowed." In fact, their salespeople are no more careful than those of any other reputable company. What they're really protecting is their own higher fees.

Exclusive listings also provide devious salespeople with a perfect cover for putting in their own underpriced offers — naturally without disclosing that they are the buyers.

Multiple Listing Service (MLS) or cooperative listings — these are really just exclusive listings that allow a salesperson to use subagents — other brokers and salespeople who are members of the local real estate board, which runs the MLS system.

When your property is listed this way, information on it is available to every member of the local real estate board, both salespeople and brokers. When you go the MLS route, any member broker is guaranteed a commission if he obtains an offer and you accept it. On MLS, your property is listed with one company, but you really have every member broker working for you. The brokers simply split the commission usually half to the selling company, half to the listing company.

Normally, your property will be listed only with your local real estate board. But if your property is near a larger board, it might profitably be listed with two or more boards. The only time you're better off with an exclusive listing instead of an MLS listing is when the salesperson actually has an offer in hand. There's no point paying the MLS commission rate when the MLS system isn't used.

Using the MLS System

The Multiple Listing Service (MLS) represents your largest single source of real estate opportunities. Across Canada in 1991 the 111 MLS systems processed 301,000 residential sales with a total value of $45.058 billion. Clearly, knowing how the MLS works and how to use it makes sense.

Each of the systems is independently run by the local real estate board, which in turn is composed of the member brokerage firms in the area encompassed by the board. The boards are voluntary and non-profit. Probably fewer than 1% of the brokers in any community are not board members; without participation in the board, it is virtually impossible for a residential brokerage firm to operate successfully.

The largest boards have extensive computerized records of both historic price data and new listings. This information is available on-line to board members for a nominal monthly charge. To impress prospective clients, some agents access MLS data with portable computers at the prospect's home.

As a buyer or seller, this computer-sorted information can be invaluable. It gives you instant "comparables" for determining what price to list your property for and what prices to offer; it keeps you up-to-date with new listings; it speeds the appraisal process; if you're a buyer, it helps you narrow down your choices of properties to inspect.

To illustrate, the Toronto Real Estate Board, the largest in the world, organizes its nearly 200,000 computerized listings of residential and ICI (industrial, commercial and investment properties), including 50,000 active ones, in three basic ways:

1. *By MLS number* — The computer-accessed listing duplicates almost all that's on the printed listing, including such details as mortgages and room sizes; it even converts metric measurements into understandable feet and inches.

2. *By address* — You can designate a street and get all the listings on, for example, Yonge Street. Or you can limit the search to specify say only properties from 1 to 200 Yonge Street.

3. *By price and MLS district* — This is the most complex search and often the most useful. Typically, you would start with fairly broad criteria. First, you might ask for all properties listed for $100,000–$159,999 in a given district. Then you would further define the criteria — say, three bedrooms and two baths, then three bedrooms, two baths and two stories, but only brick. And so on.

Average usage of the Board's three IBM AS400 systems is running more than 80,000 minutes a day from 4,045 participating terminals; 406 incoming phone lines service members' inquiries.

As MLS data includes all listings presently going back nearly two-and-a-half years — whether sold or not — it gives you a very good indication of market trends. If the listing has expired, the price was likely too high. As well, agents view expired listings as a prime source of new listings. After all, the owner has already tried to sell the property. So he's probably still interested in doing so. As a buyer, you also know that you may well be dealing with a serious vendor.

In active markets, computer-generated "hot sheet" information is essential for the serious investor. The computer hot sheet gives you the listing price, district and address, type of property and construction, the number of bedrooms and baths, the listing agent's phone number and the date and time of any open house. And you get all this information 12 hours before the printed hot sheet. So often a property is viewed and sold before noncomputerized brokers even know it's for sale.

A "prospect" system was introduced in 1986. The concept was that buyers would "order" a property with certain criteria; and as new listings fitting the order came in, the requesting broker would receive the information. Unfortunately, the program was a disaster and ended up crashing the whole system for two weeks. But it was reintroduced in a simplified form in June 1992.

Also, in 1992, the Board introduced "Trebvision," the electronic black-and-white photo transmission of listed properties to participating brokers. So now you can get an instant photo as well as written information on all Board listings.

Professional investors and experienced agents can flip through hundreds of listings a day and uncannily pick out the best properties. The photo, the price and the address catch the agent's eye at once. Any property listed at — or even below — the price of similar properties in the area makes them turn over the listing for further information. What information are they looking for on the back of the listing?

First, of course, there's the usual: number of rooms, lot and room sizes, parking and taxes. But as important, there are clues they're looking for that indicate a motivated vendor.

- *Closing date* — This is the date by which the seller wants to have the property actually change hands. Most closings are for 60 to 90 days. This gives the seller time to make arrangements of his own for buying or renting a new property.

  But some listings call for a 30-day closing or less, even immediately. Others specify a particular day. If you see, say March 27, as the closing date, it probably means something. It could be the day the seller has agreed to close on a new property of his own. It could be the day the mortgage comes due and the seller may have difficulty or be unable to get a new mortgage. For instance, the property may be highly leveraged and the seller may be unemployed.
- *Vacant* — If the property is vacant, you know for sure that the vendor is serious about selling it. He's not just "testing the market." The property may be vacant for a number of reasons: the owner or tenant could have moved; renovations could be underway and the owner has lost interest or run out of money; it could be an estate sale or a sale through the public trustee's office.
- *Price reductions* — These indicate that the vendor is serious about selling the property and is responding to the lack of market action at the higher price.
- *Agents* — After you get to know the market, you may learn to

82

recognize the names of agents who regularly list properties at realistic prices and the names of those who regularly overprice — who take listings at whatever figure the owner suggests.

- *Old listings* — Even in an active market, some homes just sit and sit. The listing sheet shows when the property was first listed. While this usually indicates a property with problems, occasionally the reverse may be true.

  Unbeknown to the owner, the listing agent may run a part-time office and no one has been able to reach him to make appointments to see the property. Or the listing agent may be hogging the listing — purposely not cooperating with other agents, so he can sell it himself and receive the entire commission. Or the property may be rented and the tenants are making showings difficult. In fact, the vendor may be praying for an offer. So why not answer his supplications with an offer?

- *Estate sales* — The owner has died and the sale of the property is necessary to close the estate. Contrary to popular opinion, an estate sale doesn't mean you're going to "steal" a property. Indeed, if the price is below-market, the reverse might be the case.

  For instance, in a recent case a home inherited by a church was listed at $99,000 rather than a more reasonable $119,900, which a comparative market analysis would have indicated. The second day, the church trustees had 14 offers. Like customers lining up at a bakery on Saturday morning, agents were given numbers. Each had one chance: present his/her offer, may the best one win. The property sold for $112,500, the price it might have fetched if listed at a more appropriate price. But it was a quick sale.

- *Power of sale* — This is one remedy that a lender who hasn't been paid can take to recover its mortgage monies: it sells the property under the authority of its "power of sale" clause in the mortgage. Again, contrary to popular opinion, the lender won't let you "steal" the property. Indeed, by law the lender is required to put forth its best efforts to get a fair market price; and courts have come down hard on lenders who haven't made such efforts.[35]

The presence of any of these clues doesn't necessarily mean you're going to be dealing with a motivated vendor. Sometimes the information was put in only at the agent's insistence; and sometimes the vendor simply changes his mind about selling the property regardless of the price and terms offered. Even if you offer the seller the full price and terms he is asking for, he is not obliged to accept.

The Listing Agreement
Across Canada, for a broker to claim a commission, the agreement must be in writing and the agent has to give you a copy immediately.

Other requirements differ from province to province. Before you sign any listing agreement, however, you should check for these key points:

Commission rate — It should be specified as either an exact amount or a percentage of the selling price. If no figure is specified, then no commission is payable in Saskatchewan, Quebec and Nova Scotia. In Ontario and Manitoba brokers are specifically forbidden to enter into agreements calling for their commissions to be based on the difference between the listing price and the actual sale price. This discourages underpriced listings and exorbitant commissions.

Expiry date — Always be sure to check your listing's expiry date. If there isn't one, or there's more than one, the agreement is invalid in several provinces. Some agents routinely take a six-month listing whether they need it or not. And some MLS systems have a 60-day minimum listing period.

Although you can cancel your listing at any time, listing agreements still oblige you to pay a commission if you sell the property within the stipulated time period in the listing. Only if the agent releases you from all obligations and agrees to indemnify you from any claims are you free to sell to whom you want without paying commission. Don't hold your breath though.

Properly priced and marketed homes typically take 60 to 90 days to sell. Businesses, commercial and vacation properties can take much longer, so they are usually listed for four months to a year.

Sometimes a longer listing is appropriate — on an unusual property or one where the owner has priced it too high and the salesperson wants time to lower it. Time after time, agents see their overpriced listings expire unsold. The disgruntled owner then lists with another salesperson who usually drops the price and sells the property.

Holdover clause — Usually buried in the fine print of the listing, is a clause stating that the broker will be paid a commission on any sale made after the listing expires, as long as the buyer was introduced to the property by that broker.

(By the way, "introduced" means that the agent or sub-agent actually brought someone to your property and they physically inspected it up close; it's not enough for the agent to have simply told them about the property, nor to have pointed it out as he drove them by it.)

Typical holdover periods are 90 days for residential and six months for commercial properties. As a vendor, you should avoid committing yourself for any longer period. Some standard forms provide for holdover clauses of one year.

Also check that the holdover clause allows you to re-list with another broker with no liability to the first broker when the property sells.

If not, you could well end up paying two commissions for selling one property.

Commissions are negotiable

Although most brokers aren't going to broadcast it, commission agreements are negotiable. It all depends on what you have to offer, the state of the market and the flexibility of the company or salesperson you list with.

Usually listings of homes and smaller commercial properties on an MLS or cooperative basis provide for a commission equal to 6% of the selling price. For exclusive listings the charge drops to 5%. The rate for rural properties and businesses is usually higher.

Large brokerage companies are less flexible in their commission structure than small ones. They can't afford to let word travel that they are cutting rates or every seller would want that advantage. Furthermore, their overhead costs are simply so high that there's little margin to cut anyway. As well, the salespeople — who frequently receive less than half the commission that comes into the office as a result of the transaction — can't reasonably afford even smaller incomes.

On the other hand, agents with small independent companies are generally more flexible. Independents are less bureaucratic and their low overheads afford them more flexibility in the arrangements they can make. For instance, to get a listing, a top salesperson with an independent might agree to "staged" commissions — say 4% if he sells the property in the first week of the listing, 4.5% if he sells it in the second week, 5% if in the third week and 6% for any sale thereafter.

In competitive markets, especially in smaller cities, agents sometimes cut commissions down to as little as 1.5% on an exclusive basis. While lower commissions may be tempting, remember that few agents will bother showing a property on which they'll earn perhaps 40% to 50% less than customary. If your agent is taking, say, 5% on an MLS listing, encourage him to split the commission — 2% to himself and 3% to the selling agent. Otherwise you're at a competitive disadvantage to other sellers.

Regardless what your listing agreement provides as far as commission structure, you're ordinarily not bound to pay it unless you accept an offer on your property. Offers usually include a commission clause above your signature. If you don't agree with the rate, you can simply ask the salesperson to change it or you tell him you'll refuse to accept the offer. But you can't change the rate unilaterally; the salesperson has to agree to any changes. And even if he forgets to include any commission in the agreement, you're still bound by the listing agreement to pay the commission.

It's useful to know that commission agreements are flexible. But before you get too wrapped up in cutting the percentages, remember that it's more important to have an effective salesperson than a cheap one. You don't save anything if the property doesn't sell or sells at a lower price. The best agent isn't necessarily the cheapest agent.

The agent's role when you're buying

An agent has more of an obligation to you when you're selling a property than when you're buying it. For unless you're paying him a fee, the agent is working for the seller. This doesn't mean the agent can do anything to convince you to buy or lease. It simply means that, because real estate commissions are virtually always paid by the seller, successful agents usually spend most of their time working on getting and selling their own listings. Buyers are secondary; agents have no hold over them. A buyer can look at properties with a hundred different agents, all at no obligation or cost. So while you're looking for your dream property, the successful agent is scrutinizing you, trying to figure out whether you're serious, or just a "tire kicker. "

If you want an agent to act as your tour guide, chauffeuring you around to numerous properties, you'll find plenty of willing takers. The brokerage business is jam-packed with low-income earners who work full-time but never sell more than a handful of properties a year; many sell none at all. Some agents boast of having shown people 60 or 70 houses before they finally purchase one. They brag about it, as if it were an accomplishment. What it shows is an unsuccessful agent with nothing better to do; it demonstrates persistence, not competence.

Before showing you any property, professional agents will want to meet with you to find out what you're looking for — and what you can afford. They may have you put your preferences down on a special form for their files, and they will evaluate your financial ability to buy and carry a property. This qualification process is essential. Many buyers, for instance, have unrealistic ideas about how much financing they can carry. First-time home buyers are notorious for expecting their first home to have all of the features of homes they were raised in. And they expect to get them at 20-year-old prices.

Once you're "qualified," the professional agent will show you the available properties that fit your needs. If a certain property meets all your requirements, the agent will start "closing" as soon as you've seen it. So why not make an offer? If your main aim is investment, fast decisions, provided they're based on solid research, frequently make the difference between opportunities taken and lost.

In Toronto, in 1989, for instance, at least one-quarter of the properties listed on the MLS system sold within a week of listing. In the booming Toronto market of 1985-1986 many homes were sold the day before the listing appeared to buyers who were kept up to date with "hot-sheets." These sheets, available to agents from the MLS system, show properties that are entered into the MLS system a day before the photo listing is published. Agents with on-line computer access to MLS have hot-sheet information a further 12 hours earlier.

Active agents will also come across other opportunities daily — such as new exclusive listings, purchasers who can't close on a property and want to assign their offers, vendors who are anxious to sell and impending listings coming as a result of a mortgagee exercising a power of sale. In other words, the agent you want to work with should be well-connected; real estate is his life, not simply a way to while away the day.

Making the most of hot-sheet and other opportunities requires working with an agent who, first of all, knows you're serious and, secondly, knows you're loyal. Anyone who boasts of having six agents working for him is kidding himself.

The agent's role when you're selling

What should an agent do for you when you're selling property? The simple answer is "sell your property." And do it in the least possible time, at the best price and with the least fuss. You should expect the agent to a) show your property only to qualified buyers; b) advertise it, taking full advantage of the local Multiple Listing Service; and c) report back to you on a regular basis what other agents and potential purchasers think of your property.

Showing should start with an "open house" for agents on the day the listing appears on the MLS system. ("Open house," incidentally, needn't be limited to houses.) The idea is to acquaint other agents with the property. Some salespeople spice up inaugural open houses with wine and cheese refreshments. These usually attract a big turn-out, but are not really necessary unless the property's exterior belies an outstanding interior that might otherwise be overlooked.

Open houses for the general public are another matter. The basic problem with an open house is that it's really impossible to qualify buyers — to find out if they're serious and can afford to buy the property. The vast majority of "guests" at open houses are more likely to be tourists on a Sunday drive through neighborhoods they've always dreamed of living in than serious prospects. Many times they openly tell the agent that they're just neighbors and wanted to see what the house looked like. Or that they are scouting out decorating and renovating ideas.

For agents, too there's a dark side to open houses. Some prominent brokers have urged their local boards to discourage or ban them.

First, there's the security problem. Though there have been few reported cases of theft during open houses, the possibility worries many in the industry. And it's a problem they naturally want to avoid. Of more immediate concern to the agents is the threat to buyer loyalty that open houses pose. An agent, for instance, may be working with a buyer for some time — showing houses, and explaining financing and the market. But if the customer walks into an open house and buys it, the agent who has been doing all that preparatory work doesn't make a cent.

The main aim of an open house is to enable the agent to make more contacts — meet more potential buyers and sellers. Rarely, in fact, does an agent sell the open house he's tending. So you could end up with endless weekends of cleaning up before and after an army of gawkers. And all with no results. Don't rule out having open houses. Just don't expect much to come of them.

Advertising is one of an agent's best tools. It takes several forms, all of which you should insist on. First, is the broker's sign. It's your 24-hour-a-day silent salesman. If you've got something for sale, you won't sell it by keeping it a secret. Nosey neighbors will find out you're moving anyway. Besides, they may provide the best word of mouth.

"Ideally," according to the Ontario Real Estate Association, "the broker or one of the sales agents should be able to match a ready buyer with each property without launching an advertising campaign for every listing other than placing a 'For Sale' sign on the property." A successful classified ad makes the agent's phone ring. Only occasionally does it sell the advertised property.

After showing and advertising your property, your agent should tell you how the market reacts to it. What do buyers and agents like and dislike. If it's price and terms that are the problem, you should consider changing them.

If you're unhappy with your agent, you can always take your property off the market. However, the agent will almost never allow you to sell it within the holdover period without paying a commission. One large broker offers a warranty that allows you to cancel your listing if the company doesn't live up to its promises. The company's promises include: providing an estimate of value based on market data; providing twice-monthly progress reports; prequalifying buyers; distributing brochures describing your property; promptly putting a sign on your property; listing it with the local MLS; and explaining to you all the ways the company will be trying to sell your property.

When you're selling a large commercial property you'll want all these services and then some. For real estate selling in the seven figure range, you should expect professionally printed brochures. And your decision to list should only be made after the agent proposes his marketing plan. In other words, how will he sell your property?

Whatever size your property is, the agent should be knowledgeable about financing alternatives and how to structure them. You don't want an agent who's lost once a sale gets more complicated than the buyer paying cash.

How to help your agent

Though the agent's job is to show and sell your property, you're not relieved of all responsibilities. You can speed the process by making your property more saleable. There are three things to look at: 1) *appearance*; 2) *repairs*; and 3) *financing*.

By paying attention to each of these points, you not only increase your chances of selling your property quickly but you can actually add thousands of dollars in value for changes that will cost you a fraction of your outlay. Smart renovations can yield the biggest returns. (Chapter 18 goes into the subject in detail.) But even little things can boost sale prices.

For example, a survey commissioned by Scott Lawn Care Co. establishes that a rich and vigorous looking lawn can add 3% to the total value of a house. Another expert estimates that you can add 5% to the selling value of a dingy home just by cleaning, painting and making minor repairs. Even if buyers know that dripping taps don't cost much to fix, the image of carelessness will stick with them and could turn a sale into a no-sale. Whether they know it or not, buyers are always looking for reasons *not* to buy. Change is simply too challenging.

Relatively minor details can add value and increase saleability enormously. Inexpensive improvements include: "dressing" bedrooms with appealing bedclothes, plants and art; creating an eat-in kitchen with just two stools and four feet of counter; hiding an offensive view with appropriate window coverings; renewing waxed floors; patching chipped porcelain; and reconnecting broken downspouts and gutters.

Neatness counts too. Clean out closets and garages — they'll look bigger. When the house is being shown, leave televisions and radios off, pets outside and children with a neighbor or relatives.

Many of the same principles apply in commercial properties. You may not have to worry about children getting in the way of a sale. But a factory floor littered with garbage, broken-up parking lots and missing light bulbs has the same negative effect on commercial buyers.

Most vendors and agents understand the importance of a good-looking property. But what they may forget is that attraction isn't just a matter of appearance. A property also has to be *financially* appealing. And that doesn't just mean a low price.

For instance, if you were a home buyer with a limited down payment, flipping through a multiple listing book, which of these listings do you think would catch your eye? This:

> Semi-detached brick house, $68,900, vendor
> must have cash, purchaser to arrange own
> new mortgage.

or

> Semi-detached brick house, $10,000 down,
> vendor to take back mortgage below current
> rates for the balance.

You're right if you chose the second one. Yet most agents put the first version in their MLS ads. It's as if they were throwing out a challenge, almost a sneer: "Unless you've got a lot of money, there's no way you're getting your hands on this one."

Selling your property yourself

Any discussion of real estate agents inevitably leads to the idea of avoiding agents altogether. In other words, selling your property yourself and pocketing the agent's commission. In normal times, up to 25% of sales are effected without agents. When markets get hot, the number of private sales rises; when it cools, the percentage shifts the other way.

Of course, the prime appeal of selling privately is saving the agent's 5% to 10% commission. It's the do-it-yourself approach. And while it can work wonderfully in many cases, there can be some sorry results too. Companies and individuals who have bought or sold (or tried to) without agents have found that moving real estate at a fair price isn't as easy as it looks. They often end up with no more money in their pocket at the end — and sometimes a lot less — than if they had paid a competent agent to do the job.

During the height of the 1981 real estate boom, a Toronto homeowner decided to save the agent's commission by selling privately. He had his house appraised by a qualified appraiser who determined the value to be $67,000; the owner then sold the house at that price. Meanwhile his neighbor listed his similar home with an agent for $99,000 and promptly sold it for $91,000. So even after paying a 6% commission ($5,460), he still netted nearly $19,000 more than his penny-pinching neighbor. Of course, it was a great deal for the buyer, a professional renovator with a keen eye for naive vendors.

In another case, the homeowner, a marketing executive with a large firm, wasn't happy with the agent's appraisal that indicated that his house would sell for $80,000. So he embarked on a $3,000 advertising campaign. After a year, he sold his home for $86,000. Was a year of work worth $3,000?

If you're selling without a broker, you'll have to do what the broker would do. That means a) *advertising*, b) *showing*; and c) *concluding the purchase and sale agreement*.

Muff any one of them and you can lose the deal. You'll also have to prepare the property so that it shows to its best advantage, as explained earlier.

Before you place your first ad, you should tell your lawyer exactly what you're doing and what services you'll need. Be sure to find out what his charges are before any work is done. Fees charged by different lawyers for the same routine work vary 200% and more. When comparing lawyer's fees, be sure you're talking about the same thing. Do their fees include disbursements? Do they bill separately each time you call them? and how much? And check their bills afterwards too. The lawyer may tell you one fee while his secretary inadvertently bills you another.

Pricing your property is tricky. Naturally, you want top dollar, yet you don't want to scare off potential buyers with too steep a price. You can invest in a professional appraisal by an individual accredited by the Appraisal Institute of Canada. They usually charge $200 to $300 for a residential property. But beware: while their training is suited to large commercial valuations, their grasp of a fast-changing residential scene is often tenuous. When prices are rising, they come in low; in a falling market, they're high.

Market comparables are your best bet. What are similar properties listed for? More importantly, what have they sold for? In most of the country, registry and land title records reveal selling prices. You can search title yourself or you can hire a freelance title searcher.

Having your property evaluated by a real estate agent can help you set your price. If it's a house, most will do it free of charge in hopes of obtaining a listing. But beware — in their eagerness for a listing, they may inflate their evaluation. They figure that once you've signed up, they can always bring you down to reality.

Besides being in line with neighborhood prices, the price you place on your property should take into account any peculiarities of location, extra features and general upkeep. Seasons count too. Home prices usually drop in winter and rise in spring and summer when the nesting urge strikes hardest.

Once you've arrived at a price, you have to tell the world about it. A sign on your lawn is your best sales aid. It should be large, professionally-lettered and face in both directions. Newspaper ads should state the price of your home and a few of its best features. It's better to run a number of small ads than one or two large ones. Repetition means exposure.

Many private ads say "no agents." But if an agent wants to look at your house, what can it hurt? Maybe one of them has a buyer. In that case, you can always offer the agent a short-term "open" listing. The listing could read "I agree to pay Y Real Estate Company a commission equal to X percent of the selling price of the property if the buyer is introduced to the property by Y Real Estate Company. This listing shall expire on _____."

Many people who show their property privately quickly realize the advantages of having an agent. You have to handle all calls, appointments and inquiries and you'll get a spate of curiosity seekers — neighbors and passersby wanting to know the price. Screening out the serious callers and visitors from the merely curious is virtually impossible. And without the buffer of an agent, you'll have little, if any, feedback.

What you should do when showing your property is highlight its positive aspects. Many good points, which aren't always obvious, can be covered in a fact sheet to be given to people seeing your property. List all the pertinent information — including size and number of rooms or rental units, special features, taxes, leases, zoning, and financing. To prove the costs of any repairs, or improvements, keep receipts and guarantees for potential buyers to inspect. Also, have fuel bills, tax statements, assessments and the like at hand. Never give out originals — only photostatic copies.

To assist in the sale, you should check out the availability of mortgage financing and get to know some of the other financing options that may come up — such as vendor financing, high-ratio insured loans and bridge financing.

Drawing up the offer to purchase is the buyer's responsibility. Your lawyer will hold any deposit and arrange for the actual details of transferring title. In a simpler transaction, such as for a single house, you may want to prepare a sample offer for the buyer beforehand. Forms are available at stationery stores, though you should have your lawyer check them first. Be sure your offer includes:

- the correct legal description of the property.
- a list of all chattels and fixtures included in the purchase price.
- an accurate recital of any mortgage or lease details. Go *directly* to the documents for the information. If you make even a small mistake, it can cost you thousands of dollars. For example, if you agree to assign liability for a mortgage bearing say, 10% interest, and the rate is higher, you'll likely have to make up the difference for the buyer.

Expect the actual offer to differ from yours. Then negotiate directly with the buyer until you reach a compromise. Or else put it all in the hands of an agent and let him handle the hassle.

At least you'll know the agent's job isn't as easy as you first thought it was.

CHAPTER 16

Single-Family Homes

Where rent controls are being tightened, multi-unit residential properties are an increasingly poor investment. In Ontario, extensive renovation of buildings containing more than four rental units is virtually
forbidden under the *Rental Housing Protection Act*. Maximum rent
increase limits have depressive consequences on multi-family investments. Converting rental buildings to condominium use is effectively
forbidden, too.

However, single-family homes make sense from the rental point
of view. Indeed, in many places, single-family homes actually *benefit*
from rent controls. And the "tougher" controls become, the more
they'll benefit.

For the investor with up to $250,000 to $300,000 in capital, properly
selected single-family housing remains the safest and highest yielding
real estate investment. And even for investors with more than that,
small residential property is often the best investment.

Here are the advantages of investing in single-family homes:

*Single-family homes fall into the category of real estate that is freest
of rent control regulation while benefiting the most from rent control.*
Modern rent controls, introduced as a "temporary" measure in
Ontario in 1975, have become a firm and permanent element of housing policy in most provinces. While economists of all political persu-
asions continually condemn rent controls as a long-term "solution"
to housing "shortages," controls have continually been "tightened"
as they're good politics.[36] "Tenants have more votes than landlords,"
explained one Ontario housing minister.

The "ideal" situation, as one NDP leader told me, is to have the
government own all the housing and allocate it to people according
to their "need." But as long as this is politically unpopular, he
explained, the next best route is increased controls over the private
sector.[37]

As a general rule, wherever rent control exists, every rental unit is subject to control. This includes everything from high-rise towers to the spare room in your basement you rent to a student during the school year.

However, many single-family homes have never been rented before, or were rented so long ago that they do not come under rent control. In either case, the initial rent you set is unregulated. So, in the beginning, you are free to rent the premises for whatever you can get, though subsequent rent increases will be regulated. The rent you get is likely to be considerably higher than controlled rents.

Furthermore, thanks to the depressive effects of controls on the supply of rental accommodation, you'll get a higher rent than you would have gotten in an uncontrolled environment. Of course, to a large extent, the market has adjusted housing prices to the effects of controls. But that's okay, because your single-family investments are always:

- *Readily saleable* — The *modestly priced* single-family home — or duplex, triplex or multi-family home that can be easily converted to a single-family occupancy — is the most liquid form of real estate investment. In other words, it is the type of property you can most easily turn into cash by selling. The resale market is as broad as the desire for home ownership is pervasive. More than 300,000 homes change hands yearly across Canada. Homes above the median price, however, are a risky rental proposition. During recessionary times, luxury home prices drop much more in percentage terms than modestly priced homes. The rents luxury units fetch, whether houses or apartments, also plunge.

  And because the market for single-family homes and other small properties is not primarily an investor-driven market, you further benefit in that 1) you don't have to be concerned with any of the special user requirements of commercial properties; 2) you're not dependent on reselling to a limited universe of investors or special users; and 3) the selling price doesn't depend on the income a buyer can derive from the property. Emotions can be given full play in the buying decision.

  For instance, if you're an investor, you're looking at the yield you can get from the property. If interest rates rise, that yield goes down — and so does the price you're willing to pay. But for home owners, there's no such yield consideration. True, when interest rates rise, fewer people can afford homes in any price range, so the demand (and prices) may lessen. But not to the extent that investment properties are affected. You're not dependent on an investor market that can be fickle and demanding. Even in real estate slumps, there are always home buyers willing to pay reasonable prices.

- *Easily understandable* — On the most basic level, all of us live in homes — that is, we all use residential space. So, as users, we can judge from personal experience which home is attractive, which isn't. Judging layouts, neighborhoods, features, the adequacy (or inadequacy) of room sizes is not an alien task. Further more, many of us have certainly been tenants, so we have some knowledge of what the landlord-tenant relationship entails.
- *Affordable and Available* — Small residential properties are well within the reach of the average small investor. All you need is $5,000 to $20,000 as a down payment for a small investment property. And even that amount can often be borrowed. Anyone who can't find the right property to buy isn't an investor; he's a dreamer looking for the impossible dream.
- *Very flexible* — In many cases, the "single-family" home is in fact — if not always in law — a two, three or four-unit rental property.
- *Easy to renovate* — Because single-family homes are smaller and the mechanical and structural systems are less complicated than those in commercial buildings, you can make large savings by doing much of the work yourself.

When investing in single family homes, you can take either the short-term or long-term view. If you have several homes, you can mix your approaches. One is not necessarily a "better" approach than another. Edward Silber, the streetwise chairman, president and chief executive officer of Counsel Corp., started his career turning over low-rent rooming houses. He then moved on to commercial real estate, trust company operations (since sold), pooled real estate loans, limited partnerships and syndications, merchant banking for developers and recently health care services throughout North America. Counsels' assets grew from $3.6 million in 1979 to more than $770 million at fiscal year end 1991. Silber started 1992 with a $17.5 million interest in Counsel.

Single-family homes include condominiums in all their various forms, and houses whether detached, semi-attached, attached, link or whatever, provided their original intended use was single family. This includes, too, the lucrative but highly specialized field of rooming houses, most of which were originally designed for single families. As neighborhoods go upscale, these rooming houses gradually revert to their original use, though often going through interim incarnations as duplexes or triplexes.

There's money to be made investing in each form. Which one you choose depends on the opportunities available in your community and how much time and effort you are willing to put into managing your investment. In high-priced areas, it's usually the only way you can get a return on rental income, but dealing with the transients whom they attract takes special management skills.

Some single-family investors concentrate on condominiums. Once you've selected the right tenant, these are relatively carefree; the condo corporation handles all major components of the property. Depending on the property's condition, houses rented to a single family involve greater property maintenance responsibilities. Converting single-family houses to multi-family use is a relatively simple way to raise income dramatically.

Other major considerations when buying single-family homes include:

Maximizing rental income — So-called "whitepainting" often creates a better return than making major improvements. For the majority of tenants, clean bright space is sufficient. Fight the common urge of novice investors to "over improve."

The simplest way of all to get into rental real estate is to rent out a portion of your own home. Usually, you can get an excellent return for the expenditure. You may be able to convert your basement into a separate apartment. Or perhaps you can build an addition to your home or convert your garage to an apartment. When you sell your home, you should be able to recapture the cost of adding the extra space. As well, in-law apartments often make a home more saleable.

You may also be able to take advantage of government programs to cover all or much of the cost of the conversion.

Ontario's Convert-to-Rent Program, administered by the Ontario Housing Corporation, is an outstanding example. Convert-to-Rent offers homeowners up to $7,000 in interest-free, 15-year loans for making additions to or converting parts of single-family houses for use as self-contained rental units. You may get an additional $5,000 if you make the unit wheelchair accessible.

Based on two pilot programs begun in 1983, Convert-to-Rent was introduced in April 1986. Its original goal of providing 14,000 new rental units across the province was largely met by year end 1991, with approximately 13,000 units completed. Annual budgets when the program started ran as high as $60 million, but over the years, spending has been scaled back. Convert-to-Rent's 1992 allocation of $1 million wasn't announced until September of the year.

Convert-to-Rent loans take the form of a mortgage registered against your property and held by the Ontario Mortgage Corporation (OMC). You don't have to start repaying the loan principal until year 11 and then it's in the form of equal payments over five years. If you sell your home, the mortgage remains as an interest-free encumbrance on the same terms, as long as the unit is separately rented and you receive prior written consent for the transfer from OMC.

In contrast to other housing programs, there are no income limits on applicants. And the only restriction on rents is that the initial rent must be established with the local program office. "I take it on a case-by-case basis," explains a program coordinator. The key is that the rents are "moderate" in light of local rental market surveys.

The maximum amount you can spend on a unit hadn't been set at presstime. But in the past, administrators point out that applicants rarely exceeded the previous $42,000–$50,000 limits. Units must meet all local zoning and building code provisions. Projects on which work has commenced before the Convert-to-Rent loan is committed are not eligible.[38]

CHAPTER 17

Junk Houses

As average home prices soar, so called "junk" houses look good to shrewd investors. Junk houses are small, poorly planned and often not well built.

Yet they can offer high returns on a small initial investment. Financing may be easier than for a better house. And you'll have more room for innovation, without risking your shirt in the process.

Take the case, for instance, of the independent investor who in 1980 bought four adjacent detached houses. He paid $35,000 for each of them; but the vendor, also an investor, took back 85% of that price in the form of mortgages. About four months later he sold two of the houses for $43,000 each, and one for $48,000. And a year later he sold the last one for $68,000 giving him a gross profit of $62,000 on the four houses. After real estate commissions and legal fees, he netted $52,000 before taxes. (The interim carrying costs had been met by the rents.) Not bad for an initial investment of less than $25,000.

To continue the tale, the last house sold was bought by an investor who already owned an adjacent home. That investor improved the junker to get better rents and subsequently sold it to yet another investor who tore it down, put up a new home in its place, and sold it for a $130,000 profit.

So how can so much money be squeezed out of four junk houses? Basically, for the three simple reasons stressed before: location, location, and location. The four homes are close to the downtown, near a park, five minutes from shopping, schools and community center. As well, the lots are large. So while many investors turned up their noses at these rundown homes, others saw why the prices were really bargains — the underlying land value.

Junk houses make even more sense when they're surrounded by better homes. For example, compare the experiences of two investors who bought into an established high-demand residential area. One

97

bought a brand new detached home with luxury features for $110,000; the other investor bought a junk house in the same area for $60,000. This year, the junker sold instantly for $95,000. But the luxury home, sitting between two junkers, sold for $139,000 — after being on the market for 16 months. So the junk home investor gained 58%, the luxury home buyer only 26%.

In a similar vein, another home buyer bought a summer cottage. On all sides though, the cottage was surrounded by year-round homes with a minimum two-acre lot size. The cottage — a rural junker, if you will — has since appreciated more in percentage terms than the surrounding houses.

Buying junkers may also offer you mare scope for creative financing. People buying down-market houses often have only a small down payment. Even if that's not true in your case, you might be able to exploit this vendor's preconception when you're acquiring the property. For example, an investor bought a $35,000 junker several years ago for only $500 down. She had been a tenant in the home for several years until she told the owner she would like to buy the house but didn't have a large down payment. Her unfailing promptness in paying her rent convinced the vendor she was a good risk. So he took his profit, not in a down payment, but in the form of a vendor take back mortgage.

Another advantage here is that because junkers cost less — and can be financed with less cash — you may be able to spread your risk. One mistake needn't be financially fatal.

Junkers are excellent too for investors who are prepared to put in some "sweat equity" to make money. That's because the houses usually have to be improved to the point where 1) they earn rents sufficient — or nearly sufficient — to cover the carrying costs; 2) you can rent them to a class of people who'll pay their rent without destroying the house.

Even so, junkers aren't a sure-fire route to riches. By their very nature, they offer a certain risk and the chance that you'll run into unforseen problems and costs. To keep that risk to a minimum you have to:

• *Check their physical condition very carefully* — Renovating invariably takes longer and costs more than you plan. The Architectural Conservancy of Ontario recommends adding 15% contingency to every renovation or restoration job.

   Every time you touch one thing in an old house, you end up doing three other things too. A renovator started stripping wallpaper on his junker. But the plaster underneath was so rotten it crumbled at the touch. So he ended up removing the plaster too, then insulating the walls, rewiring and installing new drywall all round. What started out as a $250 job ended up costing $2,500.

- *Check local zoning* — For example, in some municipalities you can build a duplex on a 25-foot-wide lot. So it makes sense to buy a junker in order to replace it with a duplex. But other municipalities may require 45 or 60 feet of frontage; or a larger lot; or they may prohibit duplexes altogether, even on a "spot" zoning basis. If you're buying a junker with hopes of eventually increasing density, don't take the real estate agent's word that the change will be okay. Check it out for yourself with municipal authorities.
- *Be realistic about rents and costs* — It's best to be conservative — that is, underestimate rents and exaggerate costs. Finally, to stress the main point, keep location uppermost in mind. A junk house holds no potential if it also has a junk location.

CHAPTER 18

Renovations that Pay

If you own a house — whether you live in it or rent it out — chances are you've considered improving it in some way. You certainly won't be alone. In 1990, Statistics Canada figured that homeowners country-wide spent a whopping $9 billion for additions, renovations, alterations, built-ins and new fixtures. And nearly half that money went for jobs costing more than $10,000 each. You might be considering changes to increase your enjoyment of your home. Other changes might help you get a better price when you sell it or help you sell it faster. Whatever the case, assuming you don't have unlimited funds, you will be facing a choice. Exactly what improvements should you make, and which ones will give you the best return?

If you have $10,000 to $15,000 to spend, how can you best allocate that money? Should you revamp the bathroom with new fixtures in all the trendy colors? Add a new garage? Chemically clean the sooty brick facade? Put in a vaulted ceiling upstairs?

Some of these choices will increase the market value of your house — and its saleability — much more than the others. But which are they?

Bear in mind, though, that increased saleability and increased market value don't always go hand in hand. Increased market value usually spells increased saleability. But something that makes your house easier to sell won't necessarily get you a higher price.

So how do you determine which changes to make to increase saleability and/or market value?

The Toronto Real Estate Board surveyed 101 of its member brokers for their views on the specific effects of different renovations. Here are some results:

TABLE 6
Upgrading with an Eye to Value

	Improving Saleability			Improving Market Value**		
	greatly	somewhat	not at all	more	same	less
Adding a rec. room	39%	42%	10%	17%	48%	21%
Improved bathrooms	52%	29%	10%	55%	24%	6%
Renovating kitchen	66%	23%	3%	42%	41%	13%
Broadloom	38%	45%	17%	10%	35%	45%
Installing a sauna	3%	34%	55%	3%	14%	65%
Central air conditioning	45%	35%	14%	19%	52%	21%
Window air conditioning	0%	26%	61%	0%	16%	68%
Adding a sun porch	21%	58%	21%	7%	23%	55%
Fencing backyard	31%	55%	17%	7%	41%	31%
Fencing frontyard	0%	34%	48%	3%	17%	52%
Storage sheds	3%	17%	59%	3%	10%	59%
Brick or stone wood-burning fireplace	4%	19%	3%	38%	45%	12%
Extra washroom	45%	35%	7%	29%	52%	14%
In-ground pool	3%	31%	48%	0%	24%	69%
Above-ground pool	7%	7%	72%	0%	3%	83%
Adding a garage	52%	24%	3%	48%	34%	10%

**In relation to the cost of the renovation.
Some answers don't add to 100%.
Courtesy: Toronto Real Estate Board

The table shows how real estate agents, who are in the market every day, think the saleability and market value of your house will be affected by various renovations. For example, it shows that 39% of the agents polled think that adding a recreation room to your house will "greatly" improve its saleability, and another 42% think it will "somewhat" improve its saleability.

But only 17% of the agents think that adding a recreation room will increase house value by more than the cost of building it in the first place. Fully 69% feel that you will either just earn your investment back when you sell the house, or else come out with an actual loss.

Therefore, building a rec room might be a good idea if you think your property's saleability is poor. But it's not such a hot idea if you're hoping to make a quick profit on a renovation investment.

Although this survey is helpful, you shouldn't take it as gospel. Like any survey, it's only an *indication* of general views. Conclusions that apply in one house, in one area, may be all wrong for another. Every house is unique; even in a row of lookalike homes, each differs. And the longer the homes are occupied and succeeding owners continue modifying them, the more they differ.

Nevertheless, some guidelines are universal.

The first general rule relates to the oldest saying in real estate, and one that still applies: the three most important things in real estate are location, location and location. A poor location diminishes the value of nearly every improvement. And the more undesirable the location, the more likely it is to erase the benefits of improvements. It's a principle often forgotten, as witness houses renovated opposite smoke-belching factories, car washes and abattoirs or under expressway off-ramps.

One renovator spent $25,000 gutting and rebuilding a rundown inner city home. Normally, that's a fine idea. But the house happens to be on one of the busiest north-south streets in the city — and the only renovation for several miles in either direction. After six months, the renovator's ads took on a distinctly desperate tone. In one ad he even admitted to his mistake. When he eventually sold it, he indeed lost money.

A second general rule is that you should avoid renovations that make your house the most expensive in your area. You or your tenants may enjoy the added features. But the price you get when you sell will likely be dragged down by the neighborhood; it won't reflect your investment.

Of course, your improvements might spark imitators. But that could take years. So unless you're prepared to wait, it's usually safer to be a follower than a pioneer.

So how about specifics? Most major renovations are now taking place in the downtown sections of big cities. In those areas, these are the renovations you should consider first.

- *Modernized and additional bathrooms.* — You don't have to go to the extremes of one wealthy matron whose home has several bathrooms nearly 20 feet square, replete with gold fixtures, antique furnishings and art work. But if you improve your existing bathroom or add a second one you would be making a wise investment.
- *Modernized kitchens* with cabinet and counter space sufficient to contain all the paraphernalia of North American cooking are also good ways to boost market value and saleability.
- *Openness and light* gets top billing from brokers and professional renovators. Skylights, sliding patio doors and enlarged windows all increase saleability enormously. "We get as much space as possible out of a home," stresses one successful renovator whose sole business is buying, then gutting, rebuilding and reselling downtown homes.

  He opens up to the rafters and down to the basement. Some of his designs include three-story atriums. Radicalism in the pursuit of openness can pay big returns, he says. Beware, though, that the extremes of the "open concept" look have fallen into disfavor.
- *Fireplaces* get top marks too in increasing saleability. Those in older homes may have to be rebuilt and the hearths enlarged to make them safe to use. Often, fireplaces built in 1930–1940 era homes were designed for only one to two hours of continuous use. Check carefully for "hidden" fireplaces in your home. In many older homes, original fireplaces have been covered over by later generations who considered them "old fashioned" and unsightly.
- *Opening up unused attic space* to create either a third floor loft-type study or simply a high-ceilinged second floor.
- *Provision for parking* — Suburbanites may find it strange, but many downtown homes don't have parking. If that's the case, you should consider ways of adding that parking. The simplest is paving your front yard. More costly is adding a basement garage. You'll need city and usually neighbor approval to do either. But parking is an improvement that shouldn't be passed up. It can add thousands of dollars to the price you get for your house, and easily make the difference between a sale and no-sale.

A third approach to adding parking is to buy or lease nearby properties. For instance, instead of renting garage space on a month to month basis, how about a 20-year lease, or even a 99-year lease with provisions for increases? You might be able to buy a right of way across a neighbor's property. Or buy the property outright.

However, adding a garage to a downtown house that already has parking space probably won't do anything but set you back the price of the cost of the garage.

An extra bedroom, particularly in a two-bedroom home, may increase saleability. But it may not raise the market value more than the cost of adding it in the first place.

On other improvements, opinion is more divided. Some professional renovators routinely lower basements in order to build recreation rooms. Yet brokers are generally sceptical of their value. "Many of them are done poorly and they're too low," complains one broker. "As a buyer, I would probably prefer to put one in myself."

Central air-conditioning is a great sales tool in July and August, but otherwise is little appreciated.

In-ground swimming pools fall into the same doubtful category. They may be *de rigueur* in southern California. But not here. You may decide to put one in for your personal enjoyment. But many buyers will see your pool only as a costly nuisance, robbing them of their backyard and peace of mind. Don't be surprised if they fill it in.

Finally, concentrate your renovation money on the interior, rather than the exterior. That's where families live. A neat, clean exterior appearance is usually sufficient.

In fact, a growing trend in inner-city areas is to present an anonymous face to the world. That way you avoid attracting the attention of burglars, building inspectors and property assessors alike.

CHAPTER 19

Becoming Your Own Builder

Ever thought of becoming your own builder? It's only natural. Real estate is an active investment. And for small investors with hands-on experience in renovating and renting property, it's often a short step from renovation to construction. Also, if you already own a junk home, you're halfway there: bulldoze it and you have the building lot.

Rather than working with what someone else has built, you get to start from scratch. Whether you're building to sell or to rent, your design maybe more efficient, economical and ultimately more profitable than what you buy ready-made.

You can build in (or exclude) frills and essentials that suit you. If you're successful, the rewards are ample. During the boom of the late 1980s, luxury infill builders were routinely netting $200,000-$900,000 for each $1 million-$2.8 million home they sold. When it collapsed, you could pick up their Testarossas for a song.

Any builder who doesn't net at least $20,000 for each $120,000 house is doing something wrong, says one successful home builder. He started in the real estate business at age 16, when he bought his first house with money saved from working on homes his father was building. He bought the house for $18,000; the rent covered all the carrying costs until he sold it for $72,000, 12 years later. Soon after, under his father's tutelage, he began building homes on a spot basis — that is, one or two at a time . Rather than buy raw land or subdivided lots in the suburbs, he built in established areas, tearing down older houses to make way for his homes. There was less competition from other new homes. More important, the neighborhoods were built up and he had a good idea of the selling price.

"You can make more money on a single home than on an entire subdivision of 100 homes, " he says now.

Some major home builders only expect to make a few thousand dollars per house. And if the market turns sour, losses may quickly sink them. But an in-fill builder with one or two houses empty can rent them to cut his carrying costs. But what do you do with a whole subdivision in the suburbs?

When you act as your own builder, you have five main considerations:

1) the way you organize your venture
2) financing
3) location
4) the design and type of house you build
5) the actual construction

If you don't pay attention to all these factors, you can still build a house. But the point of the exercise is to make a profit, not to satisfy an edifice complex.

As a builder, you can proceed in one of three ways. First, you can act as your own general contractor — hiring all the trades and organizing them, arranging permits, buying materials and scheduling deliveries and inspections. But unless your normal working hours are extremely flexible and you have substantial hands-on experience in construction, you're better off not even considering this route. Furthermore, few lenders will approve this approach. They'll insist on professional construction management. No expertise, no money.

What can go wrong with making your first do-it-yourself project a real house? Take the case of my neighbors down the street. Rejecting bids from experienced builders as too high, they proceeded on their own. First came the lowest-priced excavator they could find. The old home came down quickly enough. Then the excavators started working the site over with a bulldozer, two tracked excavators and a front-end loader. It looked for all the world like a five-year-old boy's sandcastle fantasies come to life. Burrumm! Burrumm! goes the bulldozer. After spending three weeks on what should have been a three-day job for one excavator, the excavation walls began collapsing, undermining an adjacent home. The disillusioned do-it-yourselfer then turned to a contractor to fix the mess and complete the job. And his first step was to charge more than $10,000 for driving down a ring of 18-foot steel I-beams around the excavation to support a retaining wall.

Second, you can hire a contractor who will handle the project from start to finish. The contractor will pay all the construction costs and bill you a fixed fee for the completed home. Alternatively, you may be able to go into partnership with a contractor. That way, he may forgo all or part of his fee in return for a percentage of the profits when you sell the home. The contractor's fee, which will usually be worked into the final price of the house, will be 10% to 20% of the construction cost. Do not agree to a cost-plus or percentage-of-cost contract. Agree only to a fixed price; if the contractor balks, move on to another.

A third alternative is to hire a project manager, to whom you pay a fixed fee with perhaps an incentive for early completion. In this type of arrangement, the project manager is paid solely for supervising the construction while you pay all the building costs as they come due. You benefit from the fact that the manager's fee should be considerably less than the profit that a contractor would expect to earn. Furthermore, the manager realizes no benefit by cutting corners to increase his income.

The disadvantages? You have to pay all the many bills over several months and control costs until the house is completed and sold. As well, since the manager has little incentive beyond his own integrity to reduce costs, you must insist on several estimates for every bit of labor and materials. Managers, too, will be tempted by kickbacks from trades. So you not only have to get several estimates, but you have also to have a good idea of what costs *should* be.

A variation is to make the project manager responsible for only the structural aspects of the home — in other words have him take the construction to the drywall stage and then act as your own general manager for the balance. Contractors will usually happily oblige. Most contractor conflicts with homeowners concern finicky finishing details — "Who's responsible for the 1/32 inch chip on the kitchen counter?" — that they'd rather avoid.

Before hiring or going into partnership with either a contractor or manager, check him out thoroughly. What is his reputation? How long has he been in business? Is he being sued? How much insurance does he carry? Look at other homes he has built. And before he goes ahead, you should have a detailed agreement with him on both the project and your mutual responsibilities and obligations. Your lawyer should be involved at this stage. Before you sign an agreement with a contractor, you must specify every construction detail right down to the kinds of doorknobs you want used. When you employ a project manager, there is more flexibility about construction details, but mutual responsibilities should be spelled out clearly. And you should include an override clause in which it is mutually acknowledged that the relationship between owner and manager involves a high degree of trust and confidence in the ability, honesty and integrity of the manager.

Financing often requires the greatest creativity for the small builder. If you don't have a track record, most banks and trust companies will steer a wide course around you. Good relations with an understanding and knowledgeable loans or mortgage manager can be a big help.

If you can obtain institutional financing, you will, of course, need to provide complete plans, estimated costs and all permits. The lender will then advance funds periodically, as you need them, after appraisals. These loans may be converted to a mortgage on completion.

If you can avoid financing altogether, you'll be on the safest ground. Passive investors teaming up with a contractor can be a winning combination. The investors' earnings justify larger personal loans; and the contractor can turn those loans into profitable investments.

Some investors I know have taken out loans on a demand or personal-loan basis for other purposes, then changed their minds and used the money for construction.

Taking this to the extreme, an architect borrowed nearly $100,000 to buy land and put up a new home for his family. But instead of moving in, he sold the home shortly after it was completed. With the profit from that venture, he built two more homes, netting about $100,000 on each of them. If the lender had known he was marketing the first home, it could have called the loan. But it didn't know and as long as the architect made his payments, the lender never bothered to check.

The biggest mistake you can make is buying the wrong location. Or paying too much for it. Virtually every location is sensible, as long as the price is right. When shopping for locations, look for areas that are appreciating in value. Unless you're building a rental property, choose a location that is attracting home buyers. Often it pays to work with a knowledgeable real estate agent whom you trust to scout out the most suitable locations.

The style and size of the house you build can be critical too. Though an oddly designed house in a high-demand area will usually still sell, your aim is to maximize profit, not prove a point.

The key to profitable design is "don't build to satisfy your own ego." Build to sell quickly for the greatest possible profit. Palaces plunked down amid slums will sit on the market for ages — or until they're foreclosed on by the lender.

Building to the maximum allowable coverage may make sense if you're building to hold and rent the house, but it can raise the price beyond the limits of many buyers. Fear of rising heating costs may also turn off buyers. A few years ago a badly designed seven-bedroom house sat vacant for two years while a number of four-bedroom homes built nearby sold and resold.

To avoid mismatches between house and location, research the area before you build. Study recent resales. Check out kitchen styles, the number of bathrooms and other features. Model homes are a great source of design ideas. You can usually get the builder's floor plans and elevations (what the house looks like from the outside). From these, you can have a draftsman or architect draw up working plans for the house. Remember, large and successful subdivision builders do extensive market research, so they know what sells. They also design for economy and simplicity in building. If you want to make an architectural "statement," by all means go ahead with your own design ideas. But if you want to make money, imitation is a surer route to success.

Keep in mind the basic real estate appraisal principle of conformity. This principle says that to maintain maximum value, land must be used to reasonably conform with the existing standards of the area. Only if you are redeveloping on a major scale can you go against the grain of existing development.

Lastly, there's the actual construction. How can you do it for a reasonable cost?

Says an experienced in-fill builder: "Don't trust anybody. When they see you're not a builder, they'll rip you off. Even getting several estimates won't help. You'll just get several ripoff estimates."

What he suggests, instead, is to learn as much about construction as you can before you attempt to build. Excellent information is available in books, and through night school courses you can get practical experience. For instance, in an electrical wiring course, you'll actually put in new electrical services. And a drafting course will teach you to read blueprints.

Once you know what house construction is all about, you've got the edge on the tradesmen, some of whom you'll find really don't know the best way to do the job anyway. Through experience, too, I've found that even the most skilled tradesmen are not designers. So look with scepticism on any suggestions they have in that area.

In building a house, you'll need a number of trades, probably more than you realize. In contrast to much renovation work, where a jack-of-all-trades is indispensable, new-home building involves an often bewildering number of specialists, especially in urban centers.

From start to finish, the trades you need include:

- an architect, draftsman or technologist to draw the plans and perhaps an engineer to check them
- surveyors to lay out lines, create the site plan and stake out the location of your foundations
- machine operators to demolish, excavate, backfill and grade
- block layers or poured concrete specialists, who will build the foundation
- drain and concrete workers to do the drains (and footings, where necessary), basement floors or slabs, sills and steps
- rough carpenters for framing, including framing the footings
- bricklayers

- finish carpenters for interior trimwork, such as hanging the doors, and installing locks and trim
- electricians
- plumbers, sometimes both rough-in and finish
- heating, air-conditioning and ventilation companies
- drywallers and tapers (they usually install insulation as well)
- tilesetters for the ceramics and/or marble, granite, etc.
- hardwood flooring installers
- stair builders
- railing companies, where there are elaborate staircases
- fireplace builders
- kitchen and bathroom cabinet suppliers and installers
- painters
- carpet layers
- cleaners
- waste bin companies
- roofers
- aluminum workers to do the downspouts, soffits and fascia
- caulkers
- landscapers
- paving companies for driveways and walks.

As well, you might need a host of miscellaneous tradesmen to install such things as garage doors and openers (often two different companies), central vacuum units, security systems, intercom and sound systems, cable TV, closet furnishings and mirrors. You might also want plasterers for increasingly popular interior trim details, such as moldings, cornices and centerpieces.

Before hiring any of these tradesmen, see several of their jobs, not just one or two. Perhaps they've just done work for relatives or it was somebody else who really did the work.

The actual construction — start to finish — and the sale of the house should take from four to nine months, depending on the size and complexity of the project. Your return in terms of actual dollars will, of course, vary from area to area, city to city. But if you handle everything properly, you should expect to net at least 30 to 50% on your equity on an annualized basis.

That prospect alone is enough to start you thinking about becoming your own builder.

CHAPTER 20

Speculating in New Property

In 1987, I wrote:

They're bundled up in sleeping bags and cuddled in beach chairs. To pass the long hours till dawn, they warm their hands and fill their trim tummies with steaming coffee from white foam cups. They're pretty, giggly and fresh faced.

But they're not waiting for tickets to Springsteen.

They're camped out in Pickering, Ontario, a bedroom suburb hugging Metro Toronto. And what these 80 women (and some men) are waiting for is a chance to buy one of 98 homes that a builder is putting on the market two days later for prices ranging from $120,000 to $205,000. And the homes won't even be built for another 10 months to a year. It's sort of a Yuppie soup kitchen: instead of enduring hardship because you don't have money, you endure hardship to spend money.

Condominium builders in real estate mad Toronto mostly don't even bother building model suites anymore. Instead, they do all their selling through newspaper ads and direct mail. They use "priority registrations": the first people to fill out and get the forms to the developer get the first chance to spend their money. And it works! In one project last year, the first 536 registrants gobbled up all 495 suites in a building in just one weekend at an average price of $220,000.

What we're talking about is speculation in new homes *before they have been built*. In other words, buying a property while it's still just a plan on some developer's art board and reselling it for a gain, perhaps even before it has been completed.

Mid- to high-priced condominiums and new single-family houses have been the objects of speculative attention by thousands of ordinary investors in the Metro Toronto area for the past year. By most estimates, as many as 40% of new downtown condos were snapped up by speculators and investors.

How times change. When I wrote the above, many communities were entering an amazing real estate boom. Now, in the wake of recession, the whole idea of "specing" new properties seems almost irrelevant. Except that recently some low-priced projects have been sold out with suspicious speed. In any case, unless economic law has been suspended, eventually speculation is bound to become again a factor in real estate investment. Best to be prepared.

Whether you're buying a new condo or a single-family home, the first source of your speculative profit is the same: the long lead time between your commitment to buy and the date you actually close the sale — usually when the property has been built and is ready to be lived in. In effect, you're buying tomorrow's home at today's prices. And you're counting on prices rising in the interim.

That tempting logic is, in fact, the main plank in many a developer's sales pitch.

Combine that with a small deposit, low down payments and an aggressive marketing scheme and you'll find buyers queuing to put down their money. Mob psychology is clearly part of the attraction. "Everyone's 'investing' in condominiums, so I'd better too, before all the opportunities are gone," becomes a popular idea.[39]

"It's like mining stocks," says one condo developer and speculator. "It's the professionals who are in first in the better projects — and they're the ones who're going to make the money. There's a huge amount of speculation across the board." And undoubtedly at some time during the initial marketing of a project, people will be paying "over market"; during the latter part of a boom, even doubtful projects will be snapped up.

But if you're a small investor, you can still invest in the right places and do very well indeed.

Until 1980, speculation in luxury condos was tacitly encouraged by developers. That's because the reservations and down payments they took on new projects helped free up funds from lenders; the more deposits they took, the more advances they got from the lenders. However, their attitude changed rapidly when the dangers became apparent during the run-up in interest rates of 1981-82. As the resale market the speculators counted on disappeared, many of them defaulted on their agreements to purchase. Suddenly, many "sold" apartments became unsold.

To ensure that they didn't end up competing with their own customers, developers then inserted anti-speculation clauses in purchase and sales agreements. Typically, they barred resale of the unit within six to twelve months after you have taken title to the unit to anyone other than the builder; and the builder guaranteed to repay you only your purchase price.

Additionally, developers would sell only one unit to a purchaser;

or, on a second sale, they would insist on a higher down payment. Also, the mortgagee might call a loan made for a principal residence if it discovered that it instead went to the purchase of a rental unit. Developers would also prohibit assignments of sales agreements.

Legally, the developers are within their rights in restricting sales and assignments *before* closing, says lawyer Audrey Loeb, a condominium law specialist with the Toronto firm of Widman & Loeb.

"But you can always close your deal and transfer the ownership the same day. All that it costs you is the land transfer tax. And once you are the registered owner of the unit, they can't stop you from doing anything you want to."

Besides, as a practical matter, there may be no problem, says Loeb. "If the market slumps, you're not going to be able to flip it; and if the market is hot and the developer is sold out, what does he care?"

The new subdivision single-family homes favored by speculators appeal to a different end market than condominiums: generally young, first-time home buyers. This market cares more about a detached home with ownership than glitzy downtown living.

For the investor, the speculative principle is the same: you're buying tomorrow's home at today's price.

But the mechanics of financing and the actual purchase and sale agreement are generally much easier than with a condominium. Assignment of purchase and sale agreements is more often not barred; and house builders make less pretense of being able to control your ability to resell.

On the financing side, lenders are more comfortable dealing with traditional homes than with condos. And, significantly, you're not bound up with the original blanket mortgage lender, as is the case with a new condominium.

A unique difficulty though, lies in assessing the finished community. When you buy from plans, the "community" is likely to be nothing more than 200 acres of pasture. What will it look like in a year? Or in five years?

As well, new home sale agreements are what lawyers sometimes refer to as "contracts of adhesion" — if you want the house, you sign the contract as written, or forget it. So new homes sales contracts are usually loaded in the builder's favor.[40]

Before buying either new condos or subdivision homes, you should find out if there will be a market for the finished units. This is your most important consideration. And in every case, you're looking at two things: 1) the general market for the type of housing; and 2) the specific details of the actual house or apartment you're considering buying.

Other factors to keep in mind include:

- *How much speculation overall is going on?* — If 40% to 50% of the units have been bought by speculators — and that has often been the proportion — whom are you going to sell your unit to?

  Maybe the end buyer (the actual owner-occupier) market is a lot smaller than you think. This was especially true of the downtown condos, which experienced a boom-bust cycle in the early and late '80s. No matter how excited the developers get and how many millions of dollars their exclusive marketing and sales agents make, there just aren't that many people willing to and able to plunk down $150 to $200 a square foot for downtown apartments.

- *What is the rental potential?* — Many investors make a crucial miscalculation here based on faulty logic. They see basement apartments, for instance, renting for $650 a month. If that kind of accommodation brings in $650, they reason, then a luxury two-bedroom condo should certainly rent for two, three or four times as much. In Dreamland maybe. But in the real world it's a fact that 1) there are few willing and able to spend $1,300 to $1,800 in monthly rent, whether the unit is "worth" it or not; and 2) people who can afford to spend that much on accommodation, are usually making those payments on a home of their own.

  So, despite low vacancies and mind-boggling rents in some cities, there remains a strict limit on the demand for high-rent units.

  Furthermore, when a new subdivision comes to market, fully 10% to 20% may be for rent by speculators like yourself, thus driving down the rents. In condominiums, rental units often account for double that figure.

- *Carefully comb the legal documents with the help of your lawyer.* — New subdivision agreements are notorious for clauses that may ultimately cut the value of your investment. In one, for example, your agreement to buy also constitutes your approval of any rezoning applications the developer makes for undesignated lands in the subdivision. So if he decides to build a high-rise, gas station or shopping center in the vacant lot across the street, you couldn't oppose him.

  If speculation gets wild enough, the home builders themselves don't want to get left out of the action; naturally enough, they want to reap any price increases. So they've devised ways to cut themselves in after they've already "sold" the house. Some agreements, for instance, give the builder the right to unilaterally cancel the deal after a certain period if construction hasn't begun; and even to alter its terms in relation both to the price and to the style and finishing of the particular unit. In a memorable case a few years ago, a major home builder attempted to cancel a number of agreements because the buyers didn't meet the financial standards of the lender with whom he had arranged mortgage financing — the lender was a company controlled by his father.

- *Lastly, don't be greedy.* — And don't be pressured into buying. It's easy to get carried away by the excitement and glamor of it all. Certainly, there are no better marketers anywhere than developers of new houses and condominiums: lavish literature, cheery salespeople and chicly decorated model units combine with a low down payment to make an almost irresistible package. And, in blazingly hot speculative times, there's the added allure of apparently easy gain.

    Recognizing all this, some provinces have enacted "cooling off" legislation. Ontario, for example, allows buyers of new condominium units ten days after receiving the disclosure statement and before receiving delivery of the deed or transfer to rescind (cancel) the sale.[41]

While a fast turnover is your ideal, you must be prepared for a long-term hold. And if it's not a good long-term investment, then don't buy it. Waiting for Springsteen may be the better investment.

CHAPTER 21

Apartment Buildings

Historically, for small investors, apartment buildings have been the natural "step up" from single-family homes, duplexes, triplexes and the like. Apartment buildings offer economies of scale in management and upkeep unavailable in smaller properties.

If you own a dozen single-family houses, you're responsible for a dozen roofs, heating and plumbing systems and sewer connections. But with an apartment building, you have only one set of components to maintain and repair. And because there are a larger number of apartments in one place, it's feasible to hire full- or part-time superintendents and rental agents to handle management and renting chores.

In other words, thanks to the number of units, you have the advantage of *averaging* expenses. Averaging also softens the impact of vacancies. If one half of your $200,000, two-family home is empty, you have a 50% vacancy factor. But if one unit in your 10-unit apartment building is empty, your vacancy factor is a more manageable 10%. And many times you won't have to pay anything more for the ten-unit building than the two-unit one.

Generally, the more rental units in a building — or the larger the total number of units in your portfolio — the greater are the economies of scale. For instance, a 20-unit building requires an on-site manager. But for the same salary the same individual could handle a 100-unit building at a much lower *per unit cost*. Owners of large buildings also benefit from lower maintenance and cleaning costs. Instead of hiring specialized contractors for every job, they have their own permanent crews.

Despite these traditional advantages, there are many drawbacks to owning apartment buildings in the current regulatory climate. The biggest problem is rent control, which severely circumscribes the gross revenues you can achieve.[42] Increasing revenues by upgrading buildings or units can also be extremely difficult to impossible in some municipalities. Getting vacant possession of even a six- to ten-unit building can easily take 6 to 12 months. And you may only be permitted to recover the cost of major renovations over a long period. Converting rental buildings to condominium ownership is often legally impossible in areas where it makes economic sense. Governments prefer "preserving" rental housing to promoting home ownership.

Ironically though, competition among buyers for apartment buildings can also be a drawback. Overseas investors and financial institutions remain interested in residential property. The institutions can afford low returns and taking the long view. Overseas investors are as much interested in a safe haven for their money as in immediate returns, and a large number of them have never given up the hope that controls will suddenly be withdrawn by governments more interested in creating housing than catering to popular prejudice. As well, there are always speculators in the market capitalizing on the appetite of these investors.

Nevertheless, opportunities do arise for profiting from apartment ownership, especially where:

- *Inexperienced or careless management is resulting in lower gross revenues and net income than could otherwise be obtained.* For instance, inadequate screening of tenant applications will quickly fill a building with tardy and nonpaying tenants.
- *Renovations can be undertaken that will set profitable new rent levels.*
- *Empty buildings can be renovated, refurbished and brought on-stream at market tent levels.*
- *Nonresidential buildings can be converted to residential rental use.*

The idea in each case is to acquire property valued on one basis — such as low income or nonresidential ascend to create a new higher value by increasing the quantity and quality of the revenue. But before you can try any of these techniques you'll need to assure yourself and convince a lender — that the investment is a sound one.

In deciding whether to make a loan or not, and how much to advance, institutional lenders use several criteria: a) market valuation reports; b) financial ratios; c) assessments of the buyer's net worth; and d) assessments of the buyer's management experience.

As with any mortgage loan, the first consideration is the property's market value as determined by appraisal (See chapter 3). In case the lender has to take over your property, it wants to be sure it won't incur any losses. While all three approaches to value are usually used, the income approach is only considered when there are at least four to five rental units in the building.

Lenders look at a number of financial ratios. However, each lender puts varying reliance on the ratios; and the ratios themselves may be determined by different methods, depending on the lender's individual biases, experience and understanding of real estate investment. Common measures they pay attention to include:

- *Overall or net income capitalization* — This is the ratio derived by dividing the net operating income by the selling price. The lender calculates the cap rate shown by the applicant's property and compares it to the rate of similar properties it has recently financed. In times of high demand, as in the late 1980s, rates fell to as little as 0% to 5%. Rates, especially in rent-controlled jurisdictions, now are often not as important as other factors. More important is what is the legal rent, the condition of the building and/or the cost of bringing it up to standard. As a result, "when you look at recent sales, the cost per suite and cap rates are all over the place," says one analyst.
- *Gross rental multiplier*, which is the purchase price expressed as a multiple of the annual gross rent. This rule of thumb is so crude it's given weight by lenders only if it shows a great variance with similar properties they have financed.
- *Mortgage equity capitalization* techniques. As mentioned in chapter 3, some formal appraisals attempt to separate the return attributable to the equity, from the return to debt to come up with an overall capitalization rate. But before committing yourself to a $1,500 to $2,000 appraisal, the lender may screen your application by applying a simplified version.

  One lender, for instance, assumes a 75% loan-to-value ratio — that is, 75% financing. (It uses this ratio because if it had to take over the property, that is the financing that would be typically used by the new buyer.) Then it calculates the value using a capitalization rate common to other similar properties it has recently made loans on.
- *The debt service coverage ratio is the key financial criteria*; it's roughly equivalent to what some lenders call the *default point*, the point at which the property's costs equal its gross revenues.

  The debt service coverage ratio assures the lender that, after paying all the expenses of operating the building, you'll have enough to pay back your mortgage debt while leaving a comfortable cushion in case of error. To figure this simple ratio, you deduct operating expenses from gross rents. Then divide the remainder by the debt service. Lenders generally require that you would break even, plus have 20%. For smaller properties though — one to five units — they may consider a ratio of as little as 1.05.

  For instance, assume your gross effective rents (after allowance for vacancies and collection losses) are $100,000. From that, subtract projected operating costs such as maintenance, management, repairs and property taxes — say 45% of your gross effective rents. Then divide the balance by the cost of servicing the debt you're seeking. Or:

Gross effective rent	$100,000
Operating costs	− $45,000 (45%)
Net income	$55,000

Assume annual debt service is: $46,000. So, $55,000 divided by $46,000 = 1.2 debt service coverage ratio. But say the debt you wanted to take on would cost $55,000 — $\frac{\$55,000.}{\$55,000.}$ The ratio would then be "one."

And you'd likely be out of luck.

Institutional lenders will also want to get information about your net worth. Despite all their assessments of the property, they still want to be able to sue you personally in case there's a problem.

Lenders also prefer lending to buyers experienced in property management; if you don't have the experience, you should have some provisions for professional property management.

Here's how a senior loans manager sums up his loan assessment process: "If an investor comes in focused on all those areas [mentioned above] and convinces us they have experience in the business, shows us the financial statements and has a good net worth, they'll get the loan."

Your presentation to the lender should include *pro forma* projections of rents and operating expenses. These should be as detailed and realistic as possible. And they should be supported by complete documentation: copies of the leases, utility bills and operating statements, preferably going back at least three years, from the previous owner.

If the building is vacant, or you are planning major renovations, the lender may hold back funds until you can prove you have completed the renovations and have achieved all or a portion of the rental levels you projected. In that case, you can usually obtain from the same lender interim or bridge financing until the work is completed.

In making projections and in analyzing the operating statements and materials presented to you by the seller and his agent, pay careful attention to:

- *Deferred maintenance* — The easiest way in the world to show a high net income from a building is to run it into the ground: skimp on maintenance and ignore repairs and the cash flow can be impressive. And where vacancies are high, so tenants aren't picky, this is easy to do. But eventually these repairs will catch up with you. Maybe when the roof literally falls in.

- *Inadequate or nonexistent reserves* are common in buildings with six to ten units, say lenders. Operating statements should make provision for the periodic replacement of such items as appliances, plus recurring costs such as painting and resurfacing parking lots.
- *No provision for management* — On smaller apartment buildings, the owner may be doing all the management and much of the maintenance as well. Because he doesn't pay anyone to do it, he doesn't count it as a cost. But these are real costs that investors must consider; even if they don't, lenders certainly will.
- *Leases* — Want to get a lot of financing from a lender or a good price from an investor? Just pack the property with friends and relatives "paying" above-market rents.

    But careful buyers and mortgage lenders make a point of scrutinizing the leases and the rent levels. How long have the tenants allegedly been paying these rents? Why are they paying above-market rents?

    Furthermore, if the rents claimed are in fact being paid by legitimate tenants, you should check that these rents are *legal* rents. Ask the seller for the rent history of the apartments. Also, personally check with your local rent control authority, and try to get their answer in writing.
- *Improperly capitalizing expenses* is a clever way of turning repair and maintenance costs into assets. Say the owner spends $5,000 painting the hallways and common areas. If he deducts that from his gross rental income, it obviously lowers the net income. And since most buyers and lenders put great reliance on capitalization as a way of determining value, it lowers the price (or loan) the seller could get. On the other hand, if the owner calls those expenses "capital improvements," he raises the price with a simple bookkeeping entry.

What, if after all your careful preparation, you still get turned down by a lender? If the lender cites a specific shortcoming, try to remedy it, so that your application will be more attractive to the next lender. You may even be able to bring it back to your first choice.

However, the rejection may have more to do with the lender's general policies than the specifics of your proposal. For instance, several years ago, one national lender "redlined" the entire province of Alberta. So no matter how sensible any presentation from that part of Canada was, the lender rejected it out of hand. Obviously for political reasons, it wasn't likely to have told potential borrowers the real reason for rejection. Lenders have other limits too, such as committing only a certain percentage of their funds to one type of property. Also, when interest rates are rising, lenders prefer holding off on commitments, so they can lock into the new higher rates they see coming.

In other words, don't worry too much if a lender turns down your proposal. Remember that bankers are quite a bit less than infallible. After all, these are the same people who wrote off $3.4 billion in bad loans to the likes of Poland, Brazil, Argentina and Dome Petroleum in 1988, and the same people who lent $14.3 billion to Olympia and York Development Ltd., tens of millions of it unsecured.

CHAPTER 22

Store-Apartment Combination

For the real estate investor unwilling to face the risks associated with owning an apartment building, an attractive alternative is the small commercial property — more specifically a store-apartment combination.

The main source of finding these store-apartment investments is your local real estate broker. As well, many businesses are sold privately through the local classified pages. You can also canvas the local merchant's associations which may know of businesses for sale.

Typically, these types of properties are on a main commercial street or, in a suburban area, are part of a strip mall. Perhaps the entire mall. They usually have storefronts of 500 to 5,000 square feet, one to six apartments above them and up to three floors. Many of the older buildings are in need of renovation or repair, but don't let that scare you off.

One renovator recently bought a corner store with two apartments above it for $90,000 on a main street. After spending $25,000 in improvements, he expects to get $1,800 rent from the store and $400 per month from each of the two apartments. Although this investment alone won't make him a rich man, the rents should gradually rise and the building itself will appreciate as fast as the general area.

As downtown housing areas are renovated, adjacent retail strips are similarly upgraded. Junk stores become antique shops, plumbing supply stores become bathroom boutiques and auto parts stores are transformed into jewellery shops.

Very small increments of space can yield great appreciation. Recently a 40-year-old, two-storey, street retail-apartment building was razed, to be replaced by a custom-built McDonald's. On the same street a 2,000 square-foot freestanding hamburger stand was replaced by a 6,000 square-foot convenience store.

Renovating an existing structure can yield higher rents too.

Exterior cleaning, new windows, an upgraded heating system and simply enduring cleanliness can increase your property's value.

But remember that a store that is nearly finished will usually rent faster than one in the process of being finished. Concrete floors should be capped with a new layer of cement, wooden floors patched, broken floor tiles replaced, new light fixtures added. Commercial tenants are just as susceptible to first impressions as the average home buyer.

The importance of bringing the apartments up to modern standards should go without saying. But don't go overboard, as apartments over stores almost always remain in the lower price range.

Renovation, razing the building and/or changing the type of tenants aren't the only ways to profit. You can change the use of the existing building, too. In some areas, investors have converted store blocks to prestigious professional offices.

Keep in mind that zoning regulations are crucial. Don't assume that you can do what you want unless, firstly, you have absolutely confirmed that it's legally permissible. Don't take a real estate agent's word for this. Check it for yourself. And, secondly, be sure the cost isn't prohibitive.

In one case, a knowledgeable buyer — a successful real estate broker — bought a store-apartment combination. He planned to spruce up the vacant apartments and use the rent from them to defray his office occupancy costs. But when the building inspector checked out the proposed alterations to the space, he told the owner that in order to rent them out he would have to add steel fire doors at $500 a shot, fire retardant materials between the floors, replace existing plastic plumbing with copper and install a new furnace. The total cost was so high that the broker abandoned the whole idea.

Furthermore, he found that he couldn't convert the apartments to offices because the city declared it would mean a "loss" (!) of housing to the community.

Many investors who buy smaller store-apartment combinations intend to run the store, so their first and perhaps only consideration is to find a suitable business location. Some investors take over existing businesses, improve them and then sell them on the basis of their increased cash flow. One investor ran through that process on a variety of businesses — from butcher shops to variety stores. Laundromats and dry-cleaning establishments are prime candidates for this approach. Many boast fine locations, yet are poorly managed and maintained. They cry out for imaginative new owners willing to invest money, ideas and hard work.

If you plan to rent to a business owner, you'll need to keep close watch. Lease or no lease, if they fold, you're not going to get the rent.

Remember that empty stores don't rent as fast as apartments, so screening your potential tenants is essential. Owners of shopping centers insist on examining the books of any business proposing to rent space from them. You too should demand as much disclosure as possible before committing yourself to a tenant. Keep in mind that their business is your business. Ask yourself if what they propose fits into the neighborhood.

Your tenants shouldn't overload the mix. A neighborhood can only support so many variety stores, dry cleaners and hardware stores. Only in so-called destination shopping areas, can a number of similar stores, "furniture rows," for instance, thrive side by side. Don't let nearby shopping centers scare you off. Any successful center will have applications for space from many more businesses than it can accommodate. And you may well attract them. Many businesses unable to justify enclosed center rents are specifically looking for space near the center, but not in it. There are other points to consider when buying store-apartment combinations:

- Who pays for the utilities? If there are no provisions for separate billing or charge-backs and you are responsible for all the utilities, the cost can sink you. A water bill may seem like a trifle on a $500,000 purchase. But if your tenants include a restaurant, which may even have a water-cooled air conditioner, and large families in the apartments above, your water bills can top your mortgage payments. Some trifle.

- Are you allowing enough time to fill a vacant building? Just because the vendor or his agent assures you that a store or an apartment can be rented for a certain amount doesn't make it so.

- Check all existing leases. What limitations are there on rent increases and what cost pass-throughs do they exclude? Are there "exclusion" clauses? These may limit the kinds of tenants you can rent to.

- What are the long-term intentions of the present tenants? If they will be moving on, you could be stuck with an empty building.

- How flexible are the existing financing arrangements? If there are secondary mortgages, do they have postponement clauses permitting you to replace the first mortgage at a later date?

- Is there a merchants' association? In Ontario, Saskatchewan and other provinces, the building may be part of a "business improvement area" in which there is a special assessment on local businesses and a special program of improvements to promote the area. Often this indicates a viable area on the way up. But it also means that your tenants will have additional occupancy costs. And while the store is vacant, you as the landlord may be liable for the assessment.

CHAPTER 23

Condominiums

Since being formally recognized by law in the late 1960s and early 1970s, condominium ownership has experienced great, though uneven, acceptance across Canada. Only ten years after British Columbia enacted condominium legislation in 1966, condominiums (called strata title units there) accounted for 26% of the province's housing starts.[43]

Today, an estimated 425,000 condominiums are home to 4% to 5% of Canadian households.

In condo mad Toronto — after New York City, probably the most condominiumized place in the world — condominiums accounted for nearly 21% of MLS resales in 1991;[44] and half of new housing sales. At the height of the late 1980s' boom, 13,000 to 15,000 new condos were being sold yearly in close to 100 new Toronto projects.[45] Across Ontario, there are more than 200,000 condo units.

In essence, condominium ownership (co-proprietorship in Quebec) combines individual ownership of specified units along with group ownership of common elements. Management of the common elements — everything from the roof, to parking lots to recreation centers, swimming pools and tennis courts — is under the direction of the owners (in some cases the mortgagees) in common, through a corporation (strata corporation in B.C.)[46]

Typically, residential condominiums are either high-rise apartment buildings or complexes of attached and semi-attached houses, usually called townhouses. Though townhouses need not be condominiums, "townhouse" has commonly come to stand for condominium ownership.

Both high-rise and townhouse condominiums have proven to be successful investments for many people.[47] In the leading Toronto market, long term capital appreciation as measured by MLS sales data has been excellent, though probably lagging behind undivided ownership.[48] And leveraged, modestly-priced units could clearly show positive cash flow based on prevailing rent levels.

On the plus side, condominium apartments offer distinct advantages for passive investors who can't take time from their busy careers to manage investment property. They are less prone to damage than detached properties, both from tenants and from the elements.

Also, as an investor, you are not personally responsible for anything outside your unit. Exterior upkeep and maintenance are the responsibility of the condominium corporation. So if a roof needs repair in a condominium, there should be an adequate reserve to cover the expense. You won't be faced with an unexpected and large outlay for repairs.

But any day-to-day operating costs — reflected in the monthly maintenance charges — are usually higher than for a single-family home. But at least they're steady, set in advance for a year.

Overall, there are fewer management responsibilities in owning a condominium. You're essentially managing tenant relations, not maintaining a building.

The user (non-investor) market for luxury condominiums encompasses buyers in two categories: those in their 50s or older, whose children have grown and left home; and young professionals, both singles and career couples, who have the money for luxury and a disinclination for home maintenance.

Both groups hate commuting. They'd rather be downtown, close to work, shopping and night life, than stuck in a large home in what they see as the sterile suburbs. For older owners, the condominium may be their good weather home, as they spend winters in the South or Hawaii.

What these people are looking for in a condominium is an exciting project in a prime location. It should have plenty of recreational and service amenities, from swimming pools to car washes to obsequious doormen. Security should be heavy. And the apartments should be large, well-planned and glamorous.

As in all real estate investment, location is crucial. Look for quiet, convenience and a good view. It's better to buy into an up-and-coming neighborhood rather than into one that's already established. And if you plan to hold your condo as a rental unit, buy the lowest-priced one in the most prestigious project. There are always more people with relatively modest amounts of money than there are millionaires.

In contrast to these luxury units, there are modestly priced condominiums — both townhouses and high rises. What they lack in glamor and pizazz, they can more than make up for in solid capital gains over the years. And, because there is often a better relationship between rents and carrying costs, they provide more scope for using leverage.

Experienced investors, operating alone and in partnerships, have bought a number of units in a single building or complex. The effect is almost as if operating an apartment building. But they are spared most of the headaches and hassles. And condo ownership gives them the flexibility of being able to sell the units off individually to home buyers.

Unlike their luxury counterparts, the rents for modestly priced condominiums can often yield you a positive cash flow with a 25% down payment.

In the booming late 1980s, marketers of luxury projects contended that their projects would appreciate more than modestly priced ones. In practice, all condo prices dropped dramatically. And none more so than luxury ones, where prices plunged up to 50%. Today, there are more than a few forlorn hoardings left peeling away around projects that never, probably fortunately, had a life beyond their glossy pre-sale brochures. Similarly, luxury unit rents dropped more precipitously than those of more humble accomodations.

Financing

The financing may be handled in several ways. It all depends on your income and capital, your aims, the lender's policies — and your ingenuity.

Normally, in a new condo project, the mortgage lender is the lender who has provided the builder with his interim (construction) financing and later, blanket mortgage. As units are sold to individual buyers, the mortgage is split or "fractured."

Following the 1981 real estate collapse, blanket lenders were usually unwilling to split their mortgages when they knew the buyer was an investor or speculator. But as memories of that recession faded, their attitude changed.

By 1987, they were knowingly lending to investors and speculators. And rather than counting on the potential rents to pay the loans, lenders were looking at, as they described it, "the whole picture." In other words, can the borrower afford to make up the inevitable shortfall from his investment?

Encouraged by this generous approach of the lenders, many naive buyers bought condo units that hadn't the remotest chance of achieving break-even rents. What the lenders and developers who catered to this speculative frenzy didn't forsee, of course (and as usual), was the collapse of the market. Repeating history, literally thousands of "investors" simply walked away from their existing condos and their deposits on yet-to-be built units.

High-ratio insured mortgages can still be used to cut your down payment on a condo to 5% to 15% of the total price. But this will boost your monthly payments. And in light of recent history and lender caution on non-owner-occupied units, the economics of subsidy are questionable. Mortgage brokers may be able to arrange high-ratio uninsured loans from private lenders, who will look more at the value of the property than your ability to service the loan, but expect to pay them a hefty premium.

Another financing possibility is to form a syndicate of several purchasers and then seek financing from lenders based on the collateral put up by the syndicate members.

What to Look for in a Condominium

In sharp contrast to undivided ownership of property, there are two elements to condo ownership: 1) the legal organization of the common elements you're buying into; and 2) the specific location, size, layout and condition of your own unit. And the first element is at least equally as important as the second.

Before making a decision on any condominium — new or resale — you should examine the documents controlling it.[49] These generally include the following:

1. Project documents which define the unit boundaries and the percentage basis on which owners contribute to common expenses. (In Ontario, Nova Scotia, New Brunswick and Newfoundland they're known as the *declaration* and *description*; in Manitoba, Yukon and N.W.T., *plan* and *declaration; condominium plan* and *by-laws* in Alberta and Saskatchewan; *strata plan* and *by-laws* in B.C.; in Quebec, *plan of the immoveables* and *declaration of co-ownership*.)

2. By-laws which, in the words of Saskatchewan's condominium act, "provide for the management and administration of the units, the real and personal property of the corporation and the common property."[50]

3. Rules and Regulations which deal with rules for the common elements. These include such things as restrictions on pet ownership, children, noise, prohibited activities and leasing of condominium units. (In some provinces, including Ontario and Manitoba, discrimination according to age is prohibited; discrimination for other reasons, such as sexual preference and occupation, is variously prohibited depending on the province.)

4. Management agreement the agreement between the corporation and the company that will or does manage the project on a day-to-day basis.

5. Insurance trust agreement which provides for the distribution of insurance proceeds when there is a claim.

6. Statement of recreational amenities which sets out all the recreational and other facilities that are or will be provided to the corporation and the details of whether they will be owned or leased.

7. *Budget statement* which details the estimated expenditures for the first year after the date of registration. On a resale condominium, you should see the most recent budget statement and reserve fund study.

Among the points to watch for in these documents, and from other sources, are:

- The ratio of owner-occupied to rental units in the building. Projects with a lot of rental units may experience more vandalism and careless damage than those with a preponderance of owner-occupiers.
- Occupancy restrictions and special charges that could cut your rental options. Children, pets and tenants may be barred. Or the corporation may claim the right to levy special fees for renter-occupied units, though these are usually legally unenforceable.
- The reasonableness of common area costs, especially when these are the developer's projections.
- The percentage of common area charge levied against the unit you're interested in. Is it in line with similar units?
- The possibility of future cost commitments. Usually, these can arise in a luxury building, where owners may vote for such amenities as doormen, extra security and improved recreational facilities.

As early as 1974, politicians were prohibiting condominium conversions in order to "protect" rental housing.[51] Consequently, today conversions almost exclusively involve turning non-residential buildings into residential condominiums. Though this type of conversion can be profitable, it is an ambitious project for a small investor.

As a result, the economics of renting existing units is the investor's main consideration.

On the cost side, you have to include the mortgage payments, all property and water taxes, your monthly common costs, maintenance costs for your unit, insurance, all closing and legal expenses, vacancy allowance and advertising costs. And don't forget to include the interest you're foregoing on your down payment.

Foregone interest (also called "opportunity cost") is a critical figure for condominium investors. Because of the rent-to-cost structure, down payments are often much higher than for other, comparably priced, rental properties.

Omitting opportunity costs is a common mistake among first-time investors. Yet they should be an essential part of your calculation.

In a luxury condominium with a 25% down payment, the foregone interest on a $150,000 unit would be about $219 a month. That's what you could earn on a $37,500 7% five-year GIC, compounded semi-annually. Also be sure to include the interest you forego on your down payment *before you* even take possession. Most developers nowadays require a 10% to 15% noninterest-bearing down payment for the 12 to 18 months between selling you the condominium from their plans and the date on which it is completed.

Depending on the province, you could also be losing interest during the "interim occupancy period," the six to 12 months between completion and delivery of your unit and the date at which the condominium project is registered.[52] In our example, that's another $1,300 to $2,600 in foregone interest. Since you can rent the unit during this period, the foregone interest is really no different from that you'd normally lose if you were buying an already registered unit. But you do forego the *principal paydown* you would have obtained during this period. And, as many condo investors make large down payments, that could be a significant figure. Lastly, if you were intending to buy the unit with all cash, the potential foregone interest (again, depending on your province) and the interim occupancy charges are extra costs you may not have anticipated.

On the revenue side is your rent. Realism is the key here.

Just because you're paying, say, $1,450 to carry a two-bedroom apartment, doesn't mean you'll find anybody willing to rent it for that. Furnishing your apartment may increase your rent, but in a luxury condo, tenants will expect high-quality furnishings and hotel-like service.

In the major markets, luxury condominiums have a record of wildly fluctuating prices. In boom times, prices soar; when things slow, prices plunge. For instance, two-bedroom condominiums that sold in a premier Toronto waterfront building for $255,000 to $289,000 in 1981 were reselling for just $165,000 to $175,000 a year later — a drop of 31%. Similarly, in Vancouver, condos selling for $50,000 in 1979 doubled in 18 months, then fell back to $65,000 in 1982.

An estimated 60% to 70% of buyers in the late '80s rush into downtown suites were "investors," say industry researchers.

Spanish philosopher George Santayana may have had loftier meaning in mind. But property investors would do well to recall his maxim that, "Those who forget the past are condemned to repeat it."

CHAPTER 24

Buying Foreign Property

Never again! That's the feeling many Canadians get every April after four months of snow, flu and frozen toes. That's when the temptation to invest in the sunny south is more appealing than ever. Even the occasional hurricane doesn't deter. There are mobile homes, low-rise and high-rise condominiums, detached homes and building lots. You name it. Whatever is offered, Canadians are eager for property in the Gulf states for investment, recreation and retirement, in roughly that order.

Besides climate, Southern projects often offer more space and amenities for your dollar than similar Canadian projects. And many of the condominium deals also come with agreements whereby the developer rents your unit out for you when you're not using it.

But whether you decide to buy in Florida or in any other state, beware. To begin with, the developer may only be bound by legislation prevailing in his jurisdiction. And don't be lulled into a false sense of security just because the company you're dealing with has filed a prospectus in your province. You'll very likely be on your own if you become embroiled in a feud with the developer. Though provincial authorities may rescind the developer's licence, you may not receive any compensation. And if you take the developer to court, you'll have to fight your case in the state where you bought the property.

So don't let low prices, the prospect of easy rental income or the endorsements of local financial "experts" blur your better judgement. You can get soaked. Sometimes almost literally.

Like the 6,000 people who bought property on an island off the eastern seaboard. Their adventure began when the developer bought 14 miles of unimproved, unsurveyed property and then promoted the sale of 5,000 square foot "estates" through radio ads: "Name the mystery tune and win a free down payment." Another $5,000 to $10,000 later, the "winners" owned an island lot.

But taking possession turned out to be another matter. First, it was discovered that 300 of the lots were under water; since the island was, in fact, a sandbar drifting towards the coast at 20 feet a year. There was no provision for ocean protection, no municipal improvements, roads or easements. One owner found he needed permission from 42 other owners to even reach his property. To top matters, a law permitted only one septic tank or cottage per acre. With 8.7 "estates" to the acre, the interesting question arose as to who got the cottage, who the toilet.

More recently, an estimated one thousand Ontario buyers were among 10,260 homebuyers swindled by General Development Co. between 1983 and 1990. The company and former senior officers pleaded guilty to fraud in Florida in 1990 and were ordered to pay $160 million in restitution. In the scheme, involving fraudulent appraisals, buyers were convinced to "trade up" General lots in one development for grossly overvalued lots and homes in another development.

Before buying any property outside Canada, you should:

- Investigate the developer and promoter. Their integrity and stability are their most important virtues. Speak with previous customers and take a look at the company's earlier projects. Check, too, with state authorities and the U.S. Federal Trade Commission (FTC) for outstanding complaints, if you're buying in the U.S. If there's no Canadian prospectus, inspect a copy of the property report filed with the office of Interstate Land Sales Registration, U.S. Department of Housing and Urban Development.
- Personally inspect your purchase. Nothing beats a first-hand look. Pretty photos won't reveal the junkyard or expressway behind the camera. Also, investigate such amenities as shopping and medical care.
- Buy a completed unit. Buying a completed unit saves you from surprises in construction, quality, general layout and appearance. The same goes for such amenities as golf courses, clubhouses, yacht clubs and tennis courts. In large development projects, these recreation features may be a year from construction.
- Beware of misleading names. A multinational company's name or initials may grace the prospectus, but it may well have no obligations to guarantee the project.
- Get legal advice. While some people believe that taking out title insurance, a popular purchase in the U.S., may eliminate the need for a lawyer's services, the savings may be illusory. A lawyer may be able to read between the lines and track down discrepancies. For instance, in one case, the buyer's lawyer discovered that the surveyor's description of the building was a physical impossibility.

When buying property outside the U.S., the same cautionary words apply, as well as a few others. It's wise, also, to assess the political situation in the area where you're considering buying property. Of course, this may not be foolproof. "Prosperous, friendly Cyprus welcomes tourists and settlers," read a manual on buying property abroad a year before the Turkish invasion of the island dispossessed scores of foreign property owners.

Blocked currencies, nationalization, violence and revolution can be unpleasant side effects of buying land in the wrong country.

CHAPTER 25

Profit Depends on How Well You Draft Your Offer

Finding the property that makes financial sense is the biggest step in real estate investment. But it's by no means the only step.

You actually have to buy the property — for the price and on terms that make it a viable investment. That means drafting an offer and, very likely, handling counter-offers or "signbacks" from the seller. How well you do it will affect the return you get from the investment and even its future saleability.

The offer is your promise to buy (or lease) the property; it formally describes what you want to buy and on what terms. Once it's accepted by both parties, without alteration and within the period of irrevocability, it is binding. In other words, an offer is for keeps.

At common law, an oral contract is enforceable. But most provinces incorporate in their laws the *Statute of Frauds*, which says agreements for disposing of interests in land must be *evidenced* in writing to be enforceable.

Getting your lawyer to look at each offer you make is the ideal situation. But it can be costly and impractical where time is of the essence. If you're adequately prepared, only in the case of larger properties or complicated situations is it essential for your lawyer to see the offer before you sign it. But to avoid costly mistakes in an offer, you should speak with your lawyer beforehand about offers in general. Have him advise you on what should be included in an offer, what shouldn't, and, equally important, how to handle sign backs (counter-offers), what to look out for in them, what to be on guard for and what to avoid. Alternatively, you should be able to contact your lawyer in the evening or on weekends so that you can read him the agreement over the phone. That's when many decisions on small investment properties are made. A nine-to-five, Monday-to-Friday lawyer isn't satisfactory. Don't let someone else's demand for undisturbed weekends limit your opportunities.

Though an agent may try to convince you to the contrary, there is no such thing as a "standard form" offer. Offers on the pre-printed Real Estate Board forms are usually adequate. But most of these forms have been drafted by lawyers for the Real Estate Boards, so their main concern is with protecting the agent. Forms purchased from legal stationers are often sketchy and out-of-date.

If you can't reach your lawyer and you still have doubts, you can make your offer conditional on your lawyer approving the legal aspects of the transaction. This doesn't mean that you can change the terms later, but only that you can be released from the agreement altogether.

Price, incidentally, should never be your lawyer's concern — unless he judges you to be incapable of making an informed business decision.

You may also find it helpful to take, where possible, the introductory courses in real estate that are required of prospective real estate agents.

Real estate agents are trained in writing offers. But their skills and training vary enormously. And just because an agent sells a lot of property doesn't mean he or she knows how to properly draft an offer. Agents making $100,000 a year consistently make basic mistakes.

For instance, here's how one agent we know writes an offer when the buyer is to arrange a new mortgage to finance the purchase. Her offer says the buyer is to arrange a new mortgage on such and such terms. But it doesn't specify that the proceeds of that mortgage are to be paid over to the seller on closing. When questioned about it, she says that's "understood." And anyway, "that's the way I've been doing it for eight years." In fact, the buyer doesn't have any obligation to pay those funds over. Luckily, parties to such transactions (and their lawyers) have covered her errors over the years.

So don't count on the agent even knowing how to protect you, let alone having an interest in your getting the property at the lowest possible price and on the best possible terms. The agent ordinarily works for the seller, not the purchaser. The agent is obliged only to put your offer into an acceptable form and to present it to the seller.

In practice, of course, the agent wants to get all reasonable offers accepted, so he usually works to bring both parties to an acceptable compromise. And where the selling agent is not the listing agent, he'll also likely feel a closer affinity to the buyer, whom he has worked with, than to some unknown seller.

There is no "ideal" offer, no magic wording. The basic rule is simply to avoid ambiguity and uncertain terms. In law, an agreement is not binding if it is vague or capable of more than one interpretation. The need for clarity comes up time and again in the following key parts of the agreement.

Description

A municipal address is important, but not enough. You should also describe the property with reference to the street, lot and plan numbers (if available) and a physical description of the property.

A country property will require lot and plan or concession numbers; as well, a survey of the property should be attached to the offer.

When physically inspecting the property don't take anything you see for granted. Be sure it's included in your offer. Driveways, walkways and rights of way should be described; if the property has a garage, specify that it must have access to any laneway or road.

The "more or less" clause — e.g., "ten feet more or less" — is sufficient to cover most differences between what you're describing and what you're actually getting. But you may want more precision if the property is especially valuable, or if the price is based on a price per square foot to be determined by a survey. In large commercial properties, where the price may be as much as $1,500 a square foot, the selling price may be determined by averaging several surveys.

Precise measurements can be just as important in a single housing lot. If the parcel of land is narrower or smaller than zoning requires for, say, demolishing existing structures and rebuilding to a higher use, you may have to seek a planning variance. And if you don't get it, you may be stuck with uses other than those you planned and paid for.

If a survey is involved, be sure to ask the vendor to pay for it.

Right to Assign

Ordinarily, you have the right to transfer an accepted offer to a third party, unless it is specifically forbidden. To be effective, the assignment should be in writing. However, you still remain liable in case the assignee (the party you assign the offer to) defaults on his obligations. You can avoid this risk by putting a clause in the offer releasing you from further liability in the event that you assign the offer. The danger in including such a clause is that the vendor will be adamant on his price, or even refuse to sell, if he suspects you're going to "flip" the property.

Deposit

Contrary to what you might think, a deposit is not a necessary part of an offer. A contract signed under seal is sufficient to bind you. The deposit is simply a sign of good faith on your part; it shows you're serious about buying the property.

If you don't complete the transaction, through no fault of the seller, *you will ordinarily lose your deposit.*[53] But that's not all. A deposit is not a substitute for payment of damages; it doesn't fix damages. So you can be sued for any other costs incurred by the seller, such as his legal and brokerage fees and any shortfall between the price you contracted to pay and market value of property at the time you repudiated the contract.

If your deposit is for a substantial sum — $5,000 and up — and the closing is more than a month away, it's appropriate to ask that it be placed in a high-interest-bearing deposit with a Canadian chartered bank or trust company, with the interest payable to you after the transaction closes. Usually the listing agent will hold the deposit. In a private sale, the deposit will usually be handled by the vendor's lawyer. On no account should you pay it directly to the seller.

Financing

The terms of any mortgages to be assumed or created should be spelled out, including amount, amortization period, terms, interest rate, frequency of compounding and any special clauses.

Three basic points to bear in mind: First, add up the deposit and the mortgages. Be sure they total no more than the purchase price. This may sound elementary, but you'd be surprised how many times they don't add up. "It's the most frequent mistake I see," says one real estate lawyer.

Secondly, check the compounding. The more frequently interest is compounded, the higher the effective rate. Most mortgages are compounded semi-annually, not in advance. But second mortgages are sometimes compounded on a monthly basis.

Thirdly, a *postponement* clause is essential in certain situations. Frequently, this clause is omitted by real estate agents who forget its importance. A postponement clause allows you to place a subsequent mortgage(s) on a property and give it priority over existing mortgage(s) in case you default.

Here's how it would work in a typical situation where you have a $20,000 down payment and you buy a $100,000 house with an existing first mortgage of $70,000. You ask the seller to take back a second mortgage of $10,000. Everything's fine, so far. But assume the first mortgage has two years to run while the VTB second is for three years. What happens after two years, when the $70,000 mortgage is due? *Without* a postponement clause in the second mortgage, the second mortgage "drops" down and becomes a first mortgage. Assuming you have no other source of funds to discharge the $70,000 mortgage, then you have to get a $70,000 *second* mortgage.

Whenever you're giving a new mortgage for a longer term than a prior existing mortgage, your offer should include a clause to this

138

effect: "The mortgagor shall have the privilege of renewing or replacing any existing mortgage(s) in priority to this mortgage, upon maturity of those mortgages."

To this clause, the prudent seller will add a clause to the effect that "provided that any excess of principal of the new mortgage(s) over the amount of principal owing upon their maturity shall be applied in reduction of the principal of this mortgage." Without this protection, the security of the postponing mortgage holder will be diminished, if not entirely wiped out.

Fixtures and Chattels
Generally, purchasers offer to buy *all* fixtures (items permanently attached to the property) except those excluded in the agreement. And they agree to buy a specific list of chattels (personal moveable goods). However, there's no hard line separating fixtures from chattels. So it's best to be specific. In particular, don't take for granted that all fixtures wil be included.

Vendors often have a strange sense of what's a fixture and what's a chattel — especially if they think they've sold the property too cheaply. They've been known to remove everything, from the front door to prized shrubbery, toilet roll holders, electric switchplates and even furnaces. And these are not uncommon occurrences.

When including chattels, be sure to state that they are all "free and clear from any encumbrances." State too, that any appliances included in the price are those that were on the property at the time of your inspection. Include the make and model of the appliances if you can.

For bargaining purposes, you might include in your offer all the chattels you see, whether the seller is offering them or not, and whether you want them or not. Just remember not to get hung up on them. It's absurd to lose a real estate opportunity because of a wrangle about old stoves and fridges. Never forget you're investing in real estate, not collecting inventory for a used appliance store.

On major transactions, for tax purposes, there should be an allocation of costs between buildings and land. It's in the buyer's interest to allocate as little as possible to the land and as much as possible to the buildings; that way there's more to depreciate. The sellers' interest is the reverse.

The Irrevocable Date
This is the length of time the vendor has to consider your offer before it expires. Generally, the shorter the time, the better. You want to create a sense of urgency in the vendor, so he has to make up his mind. Besides, you don't want to be forestalled from taking advantage of other opportunities that may come up.

Possession

The closing date (or possession day) is the day on which money and title is exchanged and you actually get the property. Surprisingly, buyers sometimes have the notion that the closing date isn't all that important. Perhaps they've grown so used to a lifetime of missed deadlines at school, work and play that they figure everything can be postponed with no untoward consequences.

For example, a purchaser planned paying for a home by selling securities he owned. But in order to take advantage of capital gains exemptions, he delayed cashing them in. So, on the day fixed for closing, he didn't have the money to pay the vendor. Realizing this, he offered to close the following day and pay the seller interest for one day.

The seller rejected the offer. His lawyer formally "tendered" — showed that his client was "ready, willing and able" to complete the transaction even if the buyer wasn't — and the contract was at an end. Besides losing his $5,000 deposit, the buyer "lost" the $30,000 appreciation the property had shown in the four months since the purchase and sale agreement was signed. But he did gain an understanding of the legal phrase in the agreement that said, "Time is of the essence."

Also, as a buyer, it's absolutely essential in every case that you visit the property on the closing day before money changes hands. This is for two reasons. First, you want to inspect for damage. Any deterioration of the property, other than normal wear and tear, that occurs between the time you signed the offer to purchase and the day of closing is normally the responsibility of the vendor. So your offer should usually give you the right to inspect the property up to and including the day of closing.

Secondly, if you have asked for vacant possession, you want to make sure the property is vacant, or nearly so. The vendors may be moving out that day. If they're loading up the van, you can be pretty sure they'll be out by the time of the closing. If they're not, you can ask your lawyer not to proceed or to get other assurances that the property will be vacant. Usually, vendors will be moving out when they say. But don't count on it either. In one recent case an investor closed on a property on Wednesday, planning to have it rented by the weekend. As soon as his lawyer told him the transaction was complete, he picked up the keys and drove to the house with a crew of painters and cleaners. The vendor was still packing and seemed surprised that the buyer wanted to work on the house "so fast." He said that moving was more work than he had anticipated, so he wouldn't be out for a few more days. Fortunately, it wasn't a matter of bad faith on the vendor's part. He readily agreed to refund three days of mortgage payments, taxes and utilities; the buyer was able to put off his crew till the weekend and the house was promptly rented a week later.

Problems are more common when tenants are involved. If they have a valid tenancy — and they don't need to have a written lease to have this — you can't remove them just because you bought the property. (However, you may be able to give them legal notice, depending on your provincial landlord and tenant legislation.) If they have no legal right to be on the premises, they're trespassers and it's a police matter. But this may be far from clear and enforceable.

If you know you're not getting vacant possession, the tenancies should be spelled out. What is each unit renting for? Who are the tenants and what are their leases? In light of the stringent rent control procedures in Ontario and Quebec it's essential too that you get a full rental history of the building so you can determine if the current rents are legally allowed. Otherwise, you could find yourself faced with huge government enforced rent rollbacks. Remember too, that these controls apply to every residential rental unit — even to a rental basement apartment in your own home.

Title Search
You should request a reasonable period for searching title. Though your lawyer can have the title searched in just a few days, a thorough check, including municipal work orders, can take 30 days and more.

Commission Clause
Usually, the seller pays the real estate agent's commission. Even so, the commission clause is important to you. That's because many real estate board purchase and sale forms provide that the commission is payable "on the date fixed for completion." In other words, the agent may claim for the commission whether the transaction closes or not. So make sure the commission is only payable upon the transaction closing.

As the buyer, you're not liable for the commission. But if you've made a deposit, it's your money that the agent and seller will be disputing. And if the seller turns it over to the agent, you may have to sue to recover it.

Rental Property
When buying property in a jurisdiction with rent controls, include a warranty from the seller that the rents — which should be spelled out in a schedule attached to the agreement — are the legally permissible rents. Then check those rents out yourself with the rent control authority. Don't count on your lawyer doing it.

Warranties
Provide that all warranties by the seller to the buyer "do not merge on closing." Otherwise, by virtue of legal legerdemain that continually baffles buyers, the seller can successfully claim that his warranty is worthless as soon as title changes hands.

Use Clause
If you intend to change the use of the property, be sure the offer says that the change is permitted. Be specific about your intended use.

Besides the points we've mentioned, there are an endless variety of clauses and conditions you can include to fit your particular needs. For instance, soil studies are a must when considering the purchase of any riverbank property. Toxic-material inspection clauses are advisable when you're buying vacant urban land. The convincing of recreational properties is exceedingly complex in the matter of road allowances, water rights, sewage systems and year-round usage.

If you're planning to rent or renovate, you may want to include a clause permitting you to show the property to contractors or potential tenants before closing. Speculators frequently use this clause as a cover for showing the property to their buyers.

Sometimes both the buyer and seller can benefit from letting the buyer onto the property *before* closing. In a recent sale, for instance, the seller ran out of money in the midst of renovating a large old house. Torn-down walls, dangling pipes and wiring, and construction rubble were everywhere. It looked so bad that the real estate agent mistakenly listed the house for sale as being for "land value only." However, a renovator quickly saw the problems were minor. But to get financing, he knew that many of the obvious deficiencies would have to be fixed. So he asked to get into the house before closing in order to bring it up to scratch and the seller agreed. So the buyer got his financing based on the appraisal of the already partially renovated property and the seller completed his sale. Depending on the situation, this kind of arrangement could cut your down payment sharply, perhaps even eliminate it entirely.

Any sale can be made conditional on the fulfillment of certain things — such as satisfactory financing, inspection or sale of another property. Such clauses give you great flexibility and protection. Properly worded, they can give you an "out" from the transaction while preventing the owner from selling to anyone else in the meantime. Conditional clauses buy time for sober second thought.

A typical inspection clause says that the offer is "conditional on the purchaser having the property inspected by a person of his own choosing and receiving a satisfactory report." You can show the property to your mother, and if she doesn't like it, you're out of the deal.

In many cases, though, you will insert a conditional clause, the fulfillment of which you have no control over. You may, for example, choose to buy a vacant lot conditional on the municipality granting a severance (division) of the land into two lots, thus allowing you to build two homes instead of one.

In either situation be sure though that you have the right to *unilaterally waive* any such condition. Otherwise you could find yourself losing the deal because of events (or non-events) beyond your control.

This waiver clause could be worded, ''This clause is inserted solely for the benefit of the purchaser and may be waived unilaterally, either wholly or in part, at his option at any time.''

CHAPTER 26

The Offer from the Seller's Point of View

As a seller, it's just as important for you as it is for the buyer to present an offer that is clear, unambiguous and enforceable. But clarity alone won't help you if what is clearly expressed is at odds with your idea of what you're agreeing to do.

Take the case where the vendor took back a $100,000 second mortgage for five years, bearing "10% simple interest, payment deferred to the maturity of the mortgage." After accepting the offer, the seller said he figured this meant that he would receive $50,000 in interest at the end of five years — in other words, $10,000 for each of the five years. What the clause says, in fact, is that he will receive 10% in interest over the entire five years — $10,000. For the offer to accord with what he thought it meant, the clause should have read "*10% per annum*."

Where the seller's interests obviously diverge from the buyer's is not in the form but in the substance. Buyers want a low price, sellers a high price and so on. However, it's not just irreconcilable differences over these matters that wreck potential sales. It's because sellers (a) don't always recognize a good offer and (b) they don't adequately protect themselves, before or after closing, from unscrupulous or just plain unlucky buyers.

Consider these examples:

- Hoping for a better offer, a seller rejected a $95,000 cash offer for his rental property. But when nothing better materialized, he ended up accepting a $90,000 offer that involved taking back a mortgage for $77,000 for a year. The seller — a real estate agent who should have known better — forgot a truism of real estate sales: *Often the first offer is the best offer.*

The longer a property stays on the market, the staler it becomes. (This assumes the property is listed on a Multiple Listing Service, so that all agents know it's for sale.) Rightly or wrongly, agents

144

assume a property that has been for sale longer than other similar ones must have some kind of defect. So they tend to not even show it to potential buyers. Buyers compound the problem, doubting their own judgment even when they like the property.

- In another transaction, the seller took back a second mortgage to facilitate selling his property. Within six months the buyer defaulted on the first mortgage and the mortgagee began power of sale proceedings. To protect his interest, the seller (now a second mortgagee) had to arrange new financing to enable him to buy back what he had just sold.

However, a simple clause in the agreement of purchase and sale might have enabled him to avoid the whole mess. His acceptance of the offer on his property should have been made *conditional* upon a satisfactory check of the buyer's credit. This would very likely have revealed his imminent financial troubles, and he certainly wouldn't have sold the property with a vendor-take-back mortgage.

As a seller, you want a firm deal tied up as soon as possible. So you have several points to consider in the tactics of negotiation and then in the specifics of the agreement.

As in the first example, remember that the first offer may be your best offer. Although you may eventually get a higher price, it may not be for several months, and it may require some financing on your part. Meanwhile, you may be forced to let opportunities pass, the market may drop and repair or tenancy problems could crop up.

Any change you make in the offer you receive voids it and relieves the buyer of any obligations. This is not to say that you should accept all offers "as is." But there should be some significant differences between what you're offered and what you realistically expect to receive before you reject it.

Don't counter-offer because you think that's what you're supposed to do, expecting the buyer to come back. You may very well not see him again. Indeed, "buyer's remorse" may have killed his desire for your property two minutes after he signed the offer. The well-informed professional knows that it's not worth losing a buyer for one or two thousand dollars.

Don't make selling your property a battle of wills. If your object is profit and your concession gets it, you've succeeded. And concentration on price alone can blind you to equally important parts of the deal — such as financing and the possession date.

An often overlooked part of the purchase and sale agreement that time and again gets small investors into big trouble is the *possession clause.* Where residential tenancies are involved, mishandling the terms of possession can cost you thousands of dollars.

Here's the rule: *Never promise vacant possession to a buyer unless you're sure the premises will be vacant on the closing date. And unless you're the only one occupying the property, you never can be sure.*

For example: An investor we know recently sold a six-plex to a renovator; vacant possession was a condition of the agreement. But come closing day, one tenant, who up until then he had considered a friend, balked at moving. Eventually the investor had to pay $2,000 in compensation to the buyer and inducements to the tenant to leave before the deal could be closed.

In another case last fall, a small investor was sure the family in his single-family home would leave as long as he gave them several weeks' notice. That's what they told him, he said. So he signed an unconditional sale agreement with a closing in 30 days. The day of the closing came — and the tenants stayed.

At last report, the buyer and his family were camped out in a motel, their household goods in storage, and the investor was trying to get the tenants evicted. It turns out that they were three months behind in their rent. Whether the tenants are evicted or not, the seller can expect to pay a hefty judgment or settlement to the buyer. And with a substantial asset at stake, it's a penalty of naivety he can't avoid.

You can protect yourself from this type of situation by including an *escape clause* to this effect in the offer: "If vacant possession cannot be given on the closing date, the vendor shall have the right to declare this agreement null and void and the purchaser's deposit shall be returned forthwith without deduction."

Or you could include the right to extend the closing a certain number of days in case you can't give vacant possession on the date you initially agreed on.

When it comes to getting possession, the general rule is that you can't evict tenants simply because you sell the property. Everywhere, the lease takes precedence. But even in a month-to-month tenancy, you can only obtain possession for certain specified reasons. Typically, these include wanting to move into the premises yourself, desiring to undertake major renovations and for tenant breaches of the lease — such as non-payment of rent, damaging the unit or disturbing other tenants.

There are further catches. In Ontario, for instance, you can obtain possession if you can prove you need the unit for your own use. But, in a splendid Catch 22, this doesn't apply when the property is being sold. After all, you're not moving into it. And the buyer can't apply the section since he won't be the landlord and have the right to give notice until after closing.

British Columbia recently changed its legislation to accommodate this anomaly.

Even if you do get possession, there may be a cost. In Quebec, for example, the *Civil Code* empowers the Regie du lodgement to require the landlord to pay the tenant an indemnity equal to his moving expenses.[54]

Escape clauses can protect you in other situations too. Ideally, you want a firm (unconditional) offer. (A conditional offer is one that becomes a contract depending on the occurrence or nonoccurrence of an event or the existence or nonexistence of a state of affairs.) But in some cases — such as when the buyer hasn't gotten approval of his financing, for example — conditional offers are unavoidable.

Just be sure to protect yourself with an escape clause allowing you to continue marketing the property; and if you do get a satisfactory offer, the purchaser shall have a certain time to waive his conditions. Otherwise, you shall be free to accept the newer offer.

Any such condition should be worded so that the offer becomes firm if the buyer takes *no* action to notify you as to whether the conditional event or state of affairs was fulfilled. In other words, he has to do something — typically notifying you in writing — to cancel the deal.

To protect yourself from speculators — who may refuse to close the transaction if they can't assign the offer for a fat profit — **always make all offers you accept nonassignable**.

Similarly, if you're taking back a mortgage to facilitate a sale, make it *nonassignable;* and insert a clause in the offer stating that the mortgage will be "in form and content satisfactory to the mortgagee." This means that you can put in requirements for such things as post-dated cheques and a service charge for NSF cheques — perhaps even an acceleration clause (the entire mortgage becoming due) in case of an NSF cheque.

Thanks in large part to the preaching of the no-money-down hustlers, a number of buyer tricks have become widespread. You should be particularly on guard for the following:

- *Clauses making you responsible for various costs, such as the survey, that are usually paid for by the buyer* — One audacious clause taught by the hustlers requires the "vendor to pay all closing costs." If you agree to this — and sellers sometimes unwittingly do — you are agreeing to pay for the survey, the land transfer tax and perhaps even the buyer's legal costs.
- *Subordination clauses* are a pet trick of real estate hustlers. They come into play when you agree to take back financing. A subordination clause allows the borrower to place a new mortgage "under" your loan and give it priority in the event of a default. The buyer's aim in using a subordination clause is to end up with little or no money of his own in the property, either on closing or some time

thereafter; in some cases, he can actually walk away from the closing with money.

What if you took back a first mortgage and then the buyer put a new mortgage on the property? Normally, the new mortgage would be a second mortgage. But if you have agreed to subordinate your mortgage, your first mortgage would then become the second mortgage. By agreeing to subordinate, you are reducing: (1) the value of your security, i.e., the mortgage; and (2) the equity the buyer has in the property. The less the buyer's stake, the less is his interest in keeping up his payments in case of problems.

A shrewd buyer might try to allay your fears by guaranteeing that your security wouldn't be jeopardized because the new mortgage wouldn't exceed, say, 80% of the appraised value. But buying exactly the appraisal you want is not unheard of. And even a truly independent appraisal will jeopardize your security if it enables the buyer to "mortgage out", i.e., reduce his cash equity to zero.

Subordination clauses pose no risk only where the buyer agrees that the new loan will *only* go to replace an existing mortgage, and that any increase in the mortgage amount will first go to reducing your mortgage.

- *Low deposits* — Legally, an offer signed under seal is enough to bind a buyer to an agreement. As a practical matter though, a buyer with small or nonexistent deposit may feel he has nothing much to lose if he decides not to close the deal. So a substantial deposit helps ensure that he won't walk away from the transaction, and even if he does, you normally retain the deposit, plus the right to further damages.
- *Weasel clauses* are much beloved by buyers who want everything their own way. Typically, they give the buyer the right to back out of the deal for an extended period. Examples, would be conditional clauses with unreasonable time periods for inspection of the property, approval of the purchase by a third party and arranging financing.
- *Finally, beware of the commission clause.* Standard real estate board purchase and sale forms usually say the commission is payable "upon the date fixed for completion" of the agreement. (The listing form may or may not say this.) Alter this to read "on completion." Otherwise the broker might go after you for a commission whether the transaction is completed or not. And, until 1986, the broker would have likely gotten his way in court.

However, in 1986, the Supreme Court of Canada declared that the common understanding of a listing is that it is intended to end in a sale or in nothing.[55] Therefore, a commission is payable only on completion of a proposed sale as long as it is not the vendor's fault that the sale is not completed. A "clear and unequivocal" statement in the listing that a commission was payable regardless might have altered the situation, the court said. But it decided that the standard clause in the listing agreement before it wasn't sufficient.

Nevertheless, as long as the commission clause appears in the disputed form, in either the purchase and sale or listing form, you should alter it.

CHAPTER 27

Small Savings Add Up

When you're dealing with real estate investments, you quickly get accustomed to thinking in the thousands of dollars. However, there are many more decisions involving hundreds of dollars — and less — that can spell the difference between profit and loss.

Saving, and hence making, money often means careful attention to a myriad of little matters. So here are some practical ideas on how you can save those "little" dollars in real estate investments. And little dollars carefully saved quickly add up to big dollars.

Insurance

Most investors are concerned with making sure they don't underinsure their properties. This risk can be a real one in depressed areas, where the cost of replacing your building may be more than you could get by selling it. In those situations, the best you can usually do is to find a compromise between the two levels.

However, in many more cases there's a strong possibility that you may be *overinsuring* your real estate investments. The cost of unneeded premiums doesn't match what you would lose in making a claim on an underinsured property. But why spend money at all if you don't have to?

Overinsuring comes about in two ways. First, most insurance companies today automatically increase your property damage coverage each year, whether you request it or not. The Insurance Bureau of Canada has a computer program available to its members that serves as a benchmark of construction costs for every type of property. As well, insurers use their own programs or government indexes.

Insurers say the automatic increase in coverage is for your protection. Nevertheless, the increases can be unrealistically high. So you can end up paying to protect against losses that you wouldn't incur even if the building burned to the ground. If you feel that your coverage is too high, your agent may be able to advise you on replacement costs. Or you can speak with a local builder or have the property appraised. Also, some real estate boards publish estimated replacement costs for buildings in their local areas.

The second source of overinsurance is the insistence by lenders that you insure the property to the amount of their mortgage. What this overlooks is the fact that where land value is high, the mortgage (especially a high-ratio one) may far exceed the replacement value of the building.

For instance, you own a "junk" house with a market value of $50,000. If the house burned to the ground, you might get exactly the same price for selling the property as if the house were still there. In that situation, there may be little point in having much property insurance on the house if you can help it. In those circumstances, many lenders will allow you to reduce your coverage if they receive a letter from your insurer pointing out the discrepancy between coverage and potential loss.

In one recent example, reducing coverage from $85,000 (the amount of the mortgage) to $65,000 (the full replacement cost) saved the investor $75. That may not seem like a lot. But when he reviewed his entire portfolio of homes, he multiplied savings by 10.

And that's not all. Another way to look at these savings is to consider how much property they could support and income they could generate. Even a $75 a year savings supports mortgage payments for one year on $625 of debt. Thus, with a conventional 75% mortgage, that $75 in savings allows you to control $833 worth of real estate.

In the case of larger properties, the savings are obviously greater.

Banking

As in so many things, inertia often dictates your banking arrangements. Once those arrangements are made, small investors tend to leave them in place without researching alternatives. The result may leave you in a costly rut. For example, if you deposit rent cheques in a current account and pay mortgages and other expenses from that account, you're probably making a big mistake.

One investor we know, who receives more than $100,000 a year in gross rents, had just such an arrangement. After three years, it dawned on him that something was wrong. He had paid out about $300 in bank service charges and hadn't earned a cent in interest. As a result, he switched to a daily interest chequing account. The interest he earns on the deposits pays for all his service charges, plus adding another $200 a year to his cash flow.

Shopping around for the best deal in banking services can pay in other ways too. For instance, we recently came across an investor who was ready to pay a bank $250 for arranging two week's bridge financing to cover the gap between one property being purchased before the investor was to sell another. Another bank — a smaller more aggressive one — charged the investor no fee, only the interest on the loan itself.

Application, appraisal and discharge fees vary amongst lenders too. For example, the "big six" banks don't charge application fees, as disclosure rules in the Bank Act make the calculations confusing. Other lenders may charge up to $175. Similarly, discharge fees among lenders range from nil to $200 and up.

So while interest rates, terms and privileges may sometimes be identical among institutions, remember to check the incidental charges.

Advertising

Attracting the right kinds of tenants to your property can be a significant cost. Newspaper ads are the most popular route to take in this regard, but there are other cheaper alternatives, such as:

- university housing services
- rental services that charge prospective tenants, but not landlords
- neighborhood bulletin boards such as those found at community centers and supermarkets
- internal company newsletters published by major companies.

If you continue using newspaper advertisements, beware that some papers will charge you a "commercial" rate — i.e., a higher rate — if you advertise more than one property at a time. Don't give them clues by having them bill a company or by paying with a company cheque. Using different phone numbers in ads will also avoid this problem, as many newspapers index customer accounts by phone number.

Repairs and Maintenance

While newspapers charge you more for using a company name, that name can help save you money when you are buying materials in quantity. Retailers offer volume discounts on paint, building, plumbing and cleaning supplies and electrical items. So if you're buying plumbing, for instance, first visit the decorator designed retail stores and consumer oriented lumber yards. Then go to the local dealers that the plumbers use, where you'll usually find prices 20% to 40% lower. Be prepared though to pay cash and forego return privileges.

The best way to take advantage of these discounts is *in advance* by contacting the credit department and setting up a contractor's account. If you're not buying enough to qualify for a discount, try pooling your purchases with those of friends or neighbors. Discounts of 15% to 30% are certainly worth trying to get.

When there are repairs or improvements you can't do yourself, it pays to shop around. For example a large plumbing company charges hourly rates of up to $45. Yet the very same plumbers — moonlighting in company trucks, no less — charge just $18 to $20 an hour.

Professional Fees
This is another super area for savings — again, if you shop around. There are no set fees for lawyers, surveyors, appraisers, property managers or real estate agents. Paying the most money is no more assurance that you'll get a good job than selecting the cheapest professional is a guarantee of an inferior job. Some people are simply better organized, more efficient and less impressed with themselves than others. Some major law firms, for example, seek to discourage certain kinds of work by charging a lot for it. If someone still wants to pay their price, they'll do the work. So while lawyers often charge the buyer 1% of the purchase price to close a house, many charge a fraction of that. Similarly, surveyors charge from $400 to $600 for the same job.

Take advantage, too, where you can, of lenders who may help with closing fees. Canadian Imperial Bank of Commerce, for instance, recently offered a package for homes purchased in certain communities in which it paid $549 towards legal fees and $400 towards disbursements.

Some property managers charge a flat percentage plus a fee each time they re-rent a property. But others are satisfied with a flat percentage of the rents, taking their chances on re-rentals.

There's no fixed tariff for real estate agents either. Yet most vendors accept the suggested rate without question. On higher-priced homes, there's almost always some flexibility. And agents at firms with flexible commission arrangements, and those in Re/Max type setups, regularly charge 15% to 17% lower fees than other agents.

Mortgage Discharge Calculations
A misplaced faith in computer-generated documents and in financial institutions may be costing Canadian borrowers millions of dollars a year in excessive mortgage interest charges. Here's how the overcharges, intentional or otherwise, arise.

When you pay off a mortgage anytime before the principal amount is fully repaid, there will obviously be an outstanding balance owing to the lender. The lender calculates the amount owing and will only give you a discharge when you pay that amount. If the lender is an institution, 99 out of a 100 times your lawyer will accept its figure without checking. And, indeed, if the mortgage is a straightforward, blended monthly payment fixed-rate mortgage *and you* made all your payments on-time and in full, the figures can be quickly checked against the original payments schedule you received when you took the loan out.

But overcharges arise where:

- the lenders don't follow their own schedules
- there are late payments, the mortgages are in arrears, or the mortgage carries a variable rate *and* the lenders use various "quick calculation methods," which are extremely inaccurate in these cases
- there are pre-payments that don't show up in the books, e.g., the payment is not recorded or it is recorded on the wrong date
- the lender inadvertently uses the wrong interest factor in running the amortization table; it looks authoritative, so you pay it without checking.

Take the case of a major trust company holding a $55,000 mortgage on a rental property. When the investors sold the property last year, they discharged the mortgage by paying the trust company the balance it said was owing. But they did so under protest. One of the investors was a sharp-eyed real estate lawyer who noted that the trust company's calculations showed the investors owing $170 more than on the mortgage amortization table it had provided them when they took out the loan. The mortgage payments had been made on time and in full, and there were no special provisions in the mortgage itself permitting the new calculations. At last report, the trust company had completely ignored three letters from the lawyer. The investor's next step will be to report the matter to the provincial Superintendent of Insurance.

To protect yourself from such overcharges, you should check that all pre-payments are correctly recorded and the interest factor, interest rate, amortization and term are correct.

And, most importantly, be sure that the lender calculates interest and balance figures using *daily equivalent rate analysis*. This is not to be confused with "simplified daily interest calculation," from which many of the errors arise. Without getting into the complicated mathematics of the calculations, it suffices to say that daily equivalent rate analysis is the only method by which interest due under a mortgage contract can be precisely calculated according to the contract terms.[56]

As well, for eight to fifteen dollars you can have your own amortization schedule run off by companies specializing in this. Just be sure they have all the correct information on your mortgage and your payment history.

CHAPTER 28

Investing in Mortgages

Buying mortgages is a way of investing in real estate with lower risk than if you were to purchase real estate outright. Potential returns are lower than with direct real estate investments. But your risk, too, is lower.

A mortgage is a way of securing a loan; the borrower is using his equity in real property as security for the loan. Should he default, the lender (mortgagee) can realize its loan by taking over or selling the property.

However, a mortgagee/lender isn't stuck with the loan for its duration. At any time the mortgagee can sell, trade, give away or pledge the mortgage. In fact, in some parts of the country there's a large and active market in the sale of first and subsequent mortgages, both to institutions and to private investors. As a mortgage investor, you can buy everything from a second mortgage on a $35,000 condominium, to all or part of a $25 million first mortgage on a downtown office tower.

The most active secondary mortgage market for individual investors is in southern Ontario. East and west, the market drops precipitously. Although real estate sales in Montreal create large numbers of vendor take back mortgages (called "balance of sale"), there's little trading in them.

For small investors, residential mortgages make the most sense. The amounts are affordable, the mortgages widely available and the risks are much less than with commercial mortgages. Normally, all appraisal and legal fees are borne by the borrower-mortgagor.

Residential mortgages on the secondary market are originated in three ways:

1. As the result of conventional and insured lending by institutions directly to property owners. Institutions buy multi-million dollar

pools of these mortgages. But some lenders also sell NHA-insured mortgage packages, even single mortgages, to individuals for as little as $80,000.

2. As vendor-take-back mortgages, which originate at the time of the sale as a means of facilitating the sale. The seller-mortgagee often arranges to assign this mortgage immediately on closing. But it may also be sold anytime later.

3. Finally, intermediaries often bring together borrowers with private mortgage lenders.

For the small investor, mortgage brokers are the most readily available source of mortgage investments. In Quebec, your best bet is to contact notaries. Also get to know real estate brokers and active salespeople in your area. Let them know you have money to invest in mortgages, tell them what your criteria are and you'll likely come up with some good opportunities before long. Lawyers who handle a lot of real estate transactions are another good source.

But going into the mortgage market directly is another matter entirely. Because provincial legislation governing mortgage lending has the word "broker" or "dealer" in it, many people think they can go into the mortgage business as long as they're only lending their own money. Not true. In most provinces, unless you are registered under the appropriate Act, you cannot advertise that you have money available for mortgage loans. Nor can you, as a general rule, directly lend money secured by a mortgage on real property.[57] Though vendors taking back mortgages are not specifically exempted, regulators have ordinarily ignored them, reasoning that VTB mortgages are part of the sale.

Similarly, in the regulating provinces you can generally buy existing mortgages without being considered a mortgage broker or dealer. However, if you make a practice of reselling these mortgages, especially at a profit, you may be considered a broker and be required to be registered.

The provinces without direct regulation of mortgage brokers are Prince Edward Island, Newfoundland and New Brunswick.

How does buying a mortgage differ from buying a fixed-interest investment, such as a GIC?

With a fixed interest investment, the rate you see is the rate you get. Buy a 10% GIC and you get 10% interest. But if you buy a 10% mortgage, you may well be making 12%, 15%, 20% or more on your actual investment. The key is that each mortgage is "priced" to yield an interest rate that suits the particular circumstances of the transaction.

For example, let's look at a mortgage an investor recently bought. The house was sold for $148,000 with a $15,000 down payment and two blended payment VTB mortgages — a first of $110,000 for three years at 10.25% compounded semi-annually not in advance and amortized for 25 years and a second of $15,500 at 12% compounded semi-annually not in advance, with the same term and amortization as the first; the real estate broker took back a third mortgage of $7,500 in lieu of commissions. The vendor then arranged to sell the first mortgage for $109,100 and the second mortgage for $14,800, with the vendor paying all costs.

By "discounting" the mortgage, the return to the mortgage investor is higher than the face rate. So, at the above discounts, the first mortgage is earning the investor approximately 10.5% and the second mortgage investor is earning 14%.[58]

Because private mortgage lending is usually oriented more towards the equity of the property than the borrower's credit standing, private mortgage yields are usually ½ to 1½ percentage points higher than on institutional mortgages.

However, the annual rate earned is usually less than the stated (nominal) rate. That's because, in blended payment mortgages, each month the mortgagor is repaying a portion of principal. In other words, the full purchase price of the mortgage is only invested and earning interest until the borrower makes his first mortgage payment.

So to maintain the stated rate, that portion of principal returned each month would have to be invested at rates and compounding comparable to that earned on the discounted mortgage. (The mortgage tables assume this is the case.) Otherwise, the rate you're receiving is actually lower than the stated rate.

In practice, private mortgage investors overlook these discrepancies. But they do regularly reinvest the repayments.

On short-term, long-amortization mortgages, there is even less principal pay down. So your yield is almost the same as the stated rate. Consider, for instance, the actual mortgage described on the payment schedule on the next page.

At the end of the year, the borrower had only paid off $76.37 of principal; the effective return to the lender was 13.57%.

You can usually buy conventional residential first mortgages at a yield of ¼ to ¾ percentage points above the rates paid on institutional mortgage loans. Second residential mortgages can be bought to yield 2 to 4 percentage points over conventional rates.

Whether you originate the mortgage directly — or through a mortgage broker where required — there are a number of ways of increasing your yield dramatically.

If you are buying an already existing mortgage you can't change the terms. Your only play is to deep discount the price you're willing to pay the mortgagee.

When cash is scarce or interest rates high, the opportunities are

abundant. In particular, real estate investors may find themselves holding a lot of VTB mortgages, when what they really need is money
to pay off short-term renovation loans or rising interest payments on
other mortgages.

TABLE 7

Payment Schedule

AMOUNT $15,000
RATE 14%
TERM 1 year
COMPOUNDED SEMI-ANNUALLY
AMORTIZATION 25 years
INTEREST FACTOR .0113402
PAYMENTS $176.08 BLENDED MONTHLY

Payment Number	Total Payment	Interest	Principal	Balance
1	$176.08	$170.10	$5.98	$14,994.02
2	176.08	170.04	6.04	14,987.98
. . . .				
10	176.08	169.46	6.62	14,937.09
11	176.08	169.39	6.69	14,930.40
12	176.08	169.31	6.77	14,923.63

When you're originating the mortgage, you may be dealing with
a borrower who wants or needs cash instantly for some other purpose. Besides, not everyone has the time, inclination or knowledge
to shop for the lowest rate or discount. So if your offer is not too
outrageous you could create a high yield far yourself out of a low risk.

"Bonus" mortgage loans are ideal in this situation. In a bonus mortgage, the lender doesn't advance as much money as the face value
of the mortgage. So, for example, you could take a $50,000 mort-
gage but only lend, say, $45,000.

How do you figure out what interest you're actually getting? Or
paying, if you're the mortgagor?

Usually, the term and amortization aren't the same. When that's
the case, use your amortization tables to determine the regular monthly
payments of principal and interest due for the full stated amount of
the mortgage. Then divide the total amount of the bonus by the number of payments in the term of the mortgage. Add that figure to the
regular monthly payment. Then look up the interest rate at the discounted amount that requires the monthly payment you've just added
up. This will show you the approximate interest rate you're earning

(or paying) on the money actually advanced. The accuracy depends on how detailed your tables are.

To take a concrete example, assume the $50,000 mortgage above was amortized for 25 years with a three-year term and carried a face rate of 12% calculated semi-annually not in advance. The monthly blended payment is $515.95; the $5,000 bonus divided by 36 (the number of payments over three years) is $138.88. Added together, they total $654.83.

Using the amortization tables, you will find that the closest equivalent monthly payment for that amortization period for a $45,000 loan is $655.71 — an interest rate of approximately 17.875%.

Another strategy for creating safe high yields is to concentrate on buying discounted small second and even third mortgages. The key is that for what is really a nominal fee for the mortgage seller, you can create a high yield. For instance, assume a seller takes back an $8,000 second mortgage amortized for 25 years with a one year term at 12.5%. By discounting that mortgage merely $375 — that is, buying it for $7,625 — you can create an 18% yield; for a $500 discount, your yield would be 20%.

Mortgage lending doesn't have to be long term either. In some circumstances, you can get a handsome return quickly. Take the case where a buyer, for reasons beyond his control, can't get the financing he needs by the closing date. Perhaps a mortgage broker hasn't lived up to his commitment. Or the lender changed its mind. Or maybe the buyer had a partner who, at the last moment, decided not to contribute his share to the down payment.

Whatever the reason, the buyer has a closing to meet — and no money. If he can't get the seller to delay the closing, he stands to lose the property and faces a possible lawsuit for damages launched by the seller. If you can loan the money secured by a mortgage for just a short time, the buyer can then arrange other financing. There's no reason, for example, you couldn't lend for a three-month term.

Last year, a buyer in such a predicament turned to a private lender and got a bonused $188,000 first mortgage at 10% on exactly that basis. So when the mortgagor (borrower) paid off the loan one month later with the proceeds of a new long-term first mortgage, the effective yield to the lender on an annualized basis was approximately 30%.

When you are originating the loan directly, you also have an opportunity to boost your return. Besides setting the rate, you can include special penalty charges for late payments, discharge fees, inspection fees and the like. Of course, if you get carried away, the borrower may simply go elsewhere. Or you could risk violating laws on unconscionable transactions.

It is a truism that higher returns mean higher risks. And mortgages *are* riskier than institutional investments. So you have to know how to assess the quality of the mortgage.

Experienced mortgage investors look at three factors: equity, the mortgagor's covenant, and the property.

Equity is the value of the property after the mortgages. On a sale, it means the buyer's down payment; where the owner is placing a mortgage on a property he already owns, equity is the difference between the property's value and the amount of the mortgages.

The equity is your safety cushion in case the mortgage turns sour and you end up with the property. It provides the cash to cover your costs in taking over and reselling the property; and it also safeguards you if the property value drops.

It follows then that *the higher the ratio of loan to value, the greater is your risk.*

Consider what might happen if the equity were low. Say someone buys an $80,000 house with 10% down — $8,000. Payment on a $72,000 mortgage at 10% amortized for 25 years comes to $656 a month, plus perhaps $70 monthly for taxes.

If the buyer defaults on the payments and you, as the mortgagee, have to take the house back, what could happen?

If the borrower disputes your action, it could take six to twelve months before you get possession. So the mortgage and tax arrears alone would come to at least $4,400. Plus you'll have legal bills and perhaps repairs, sometimes to fix intentional damage. Even if you sell the house for its purchase price of $80,000, you'll likely incur real estate commissions of $4,000 to $4,800. As you can see, on a default you can easily eat up the buyer's equity and still end up out-of-pocket.

Equity can be similarly wiped out if property values drop. Many lenders found themselves in exactly that situation after the collapse of inflated values following the 1981 and 1988–89 real estate booms.

In 1981, a speculator bought a small bungalow for $145,000 with $20,000 down, assumed an existing $100,000 mortgage and gave the seller a $25,000 take-back second mortgage. The "spec" anticipated quickly reselling the property for $175,000 to $180,000. But the market collapsed and he defaulted on his first mortgage. So the former owner took over the first mortgage payments and taxes and exercised his power of sale under his take-back mortgage. But in the suddenly depressed market, he could only get $128,000 for the house. Real estate commissions, holding costs and legal fees ate up $12,000 of that. So the $25,000 mortgage he had taken back turned out to be worthless, plus he lost another $4,000.

The situation repeated itself in the 1990–91 collapse. Home prices in many southern Ontario neighborhoods, for instance, plunged 40% from their pre-recession heights. Consequently, lenders, sellers and investors holding mortgages for anything over 70% of boom-time prices risked ending up with worthless paper.

As a minimum safety margin, mortgage brokers today suggest that borrowers have at least 15% equity in any property. Of course, you're free to accept riskier deals. Given the right circumstances, a mortgage with 10% down may be worth the risk as long as: 1) you're not putting all your money into the one investment; and, 2) you're absolutely positive about the value of the property.

You should never lend on a first mortgage beyond 70% to 75% of value. If you do and there's a default, your entire investment is at risk, not just the high-risk portion. And remember that you can't insure any of this risk, as mortgage insurance is restricted to institutional mortgages.

Brokers emphasize, too, that the percentage of equity — not the absolute amount of money invested — is the more important criterion. Thus a buyer with a $10,000 down payment in a $60,000 "junker" is usually a better bet than the buyer with the same amount of cash in a $100,000 suburban bungalow. The "junker" owner has a 16.6% down payment, the suburban owner just 10% down.

As you would expect, first mortgages are generally less risky than subsequent mortgages. Few investors are willing to go past second mortgages. Second and other subsequent mortgagees usually have less of an equity cushion and if there is a default in a prior mortgage(s), they have to make the payments on those mortgages to protect the value of their mortgage.

But while there's more of a risk with second and subsequent mortgages, your risk depends more on the total loan-to-value ratio than the precedence of the mortgages. As long as there's enough equity in the property, after the mortgages, to reimburse your recovery costs, it's not much riskier to hold a second mortgage than a first.

Equity, remember, is the unencumbered portion of the fair market value of the property retained by the owner. In other words, equity is how much the property is worth after any mortgages or other charges against it are subtracted. It's important to remember that *mortgages don't increase a property's value or the owner's equity.*

This is to forewarn you of mortgage brokers or borrowers who may try to convince you there's more equity in the property than there really is because of the total sum of the mortgages.

To illustrate: you are buying a second mortgage on a property where the owner has offered 10% as a down payment; there's also going to be a third mortgage on the property for 10% of the selling price. Unless the value of the property increases dramatically by closing, the buyer's equity is 10% — not 20%.

The only comfort a subsequent mortgage offers you is that in case the borrower defaults on your loan, the subsequent lender might keep your payments up to date to avoid losing his interest in the property.

The next criterion is the creditworthiness of the buyer or owner.

Though you're not bound to the standard formulas that institutional lenders apply, you should at least get proof of the buyer's income and stability. Request a letter from his employer that states his or her present and projected income. If the buyer is self-employed, you could ask for a statement of assets and liabilities or for a look at their books. Also, get a credit check through your own banker.

Keep in mind that mortgage brokers as a rule do not do credit checks on the mortgagors.

Urban bank managers tend to favor employees over self-employed people. But in rural areas, "I'd much prefer doing a deal with a self-employed plumber than with a government employee," says a former president of the Ontario Mortgage Brokers Association.

Finally, before committing yourself, you should examine the accepted agreement of purchase and sale. This will give you some assurance that a real transaction is taking place and that the financing relates to the agreement between the parties. It should also indicate if any other financing is being assumed. On closing, too, the lawyer acting for you should be alerted to be aware of any "hidden" mortgages being registered and should have directions not to advance funds if this is the case.

You should always look, too, at the property. It is your ultimate security. There you have three considerations:

1. Is it worth the purchase price? Compare the alleged sale price to the prices paid for similar properties in the neighborhood. It should be consistent. Physically inspect the property if you can. Or at least, visit it, walk around it.

What continually comes up in mortgage scams is that if the deceived investors had actually taken the time to visit the property, they would have immediately suspected that the mortgage far exceeded what the property was worth.

In this regard, be extremely skeptical of private sales. Conspirators may arrange a "sale", get mortgage money for part of the "purchase" price and then split the proceeds between them. Agents, too, aren't above similar arrangements — for instance, hiding vendor-take-back financing in separate side agreements so that the buyer gets the property for no down payment.

2. How fast will you be able to sell it in case there's a default? A marketable conventional property consistent with the neighborhood it's in is always the least risk.

3. If it's a rental property, will the rents be able to support the carrying costs? Be sure the current rent schedule makes sense in light of local conditions. Could you get the same rents if you ended up with the building?

Beware that in some jurisdictions you will end up as the landlord if you have to take over from a defaulting mortgagor. As a "mortgagee in possession," you will then be under all the obligations of landlord and tenant legislation, such as notice, property standards and the like. So if the borrower couldn't pay you because he had a building, or even a single-family home, full of deadbeat tenants, they'll then be your tenants.

If a lawyer is originating the mortgage, take special care that you are actually buying a mortgage, not paying off the lawyer's bad investments. Diverting mortgage funds is one of the most popular routes taken by disbarred lawyers.

A lawyer convicted in 1982 of stealing more than $2 million over a five-year period would type out mortgage papers in the name of his client, using the names and addresses of former clients. Then he would cut the registry stamp from the old mortgage papers and paste it onto the new "mortgage" documents and photocopy them, sending the photocopies to the clients, who would believe they held a valid registered mortgage. The lawyer then kept up the interest payments to the clients and paid off the "mortgages" when they came due. But, as in all such schemes, eventually the outgo on the phony mortgages couldn't be matched by new money.[59]

Just as you can leverage stock investment, mortgage investment, too, can be leveraged by borrowing money to buy the mortgages. You can leverage with any borrowed funds. But to make the exercise practicable and profitable, you will have to use funds that are 1) borrowed at the lowest possible interest rate. So, for example, taking out a personal loan, at say, 2% over prime, to buy a mortgage yielding the same rate is pointless; and 2) repayable over a period of time or in a manner so that your regular loan repayments are lower than your regular mortgage payments.

A combination of unborrowed money and funds borrowed at relatively low rates — as on a mortgage or interest-only line of credit — makes the most sense. Or you might be able to borrow against the collateral in any mortgages you already hold, including ones you took back to help sell your own properties. Or you might mortgage property you own. Say you have $50,000 to invest. To that, you add $100,000 from mortgaging property you own.

Cost of borrowed $100,000*	Yield on $150,000 you're lending**
$979.76 monthly payments	$ 1,760.81 monthly payments
× 12	× 12
$11,757.12	$21,129.72
− 700.00 principal repayment	− 750.00 principal repayment
$11,057.12	$ 20,379.72
	− 11,057.12
	$ 9,322.60

* assumes 12% interest, 25-year amortization
**assumes 14% interest, 25-year amortization

So after one year you end up with $9,322.60 in interest on a $50,000 equity investment. That's a pre-tax return on equity of 18.65%.

Nevertheless, most brokers warn against going overboard using borrowed money. "The guys I know who are doing it have large bank lines and never leverage more than three to one," says one mortgage broker veteran.

Beware, too, that using a line of credit — or other variable rate money — to buy long-term, fixed-interest investments can be a recipe for disaster if interest rates rise. Borrowing short and lending long is the secret behind many a failed financier.

Mortgages are less liquid than stocks and bonds but they can usually be resold through mortgage brokers.

If you might be reselling the mortgage, you should restrict yourself to mortgages with short fixed terms — one to three years with few or no prepayment clauses. There should be at least 15% equity, a strong covenant and the property should be easily marketable.

One mortgage broker sums up the pluses and minuses of investing in mortgages: "You can't get around aggravation. But you are getting a better rate than you can get at a bank. Just don't look for pie-in-the-sky deals and not expect problems."

Indirect Mortgage Investments

Each step you move away from directly owning real estate, the more what you're buying resembles a fixed-interest security rather than a vehicle for entrepreneurial wealth-building. What you gain in safety and liquidity, you lose in return. Indirect mortgage investments include the following:

CMHC-Insured Mortgage-backed Securities
Mortgage-backed securities (MBS), first introduced in Canada in 1985 by privately owned GMC Investors, are a form of securities representing an interest in pools of mortgages. Since 1986, when CMHC

inaugurated its own MBS program, the mortgages in those pools have been insured through the National Housing Act (NHA), which provides a 100% guarantee of timely payment to investors in case the underlying mortgages go into default.

After creating the MBS, nicknamed Cannie Maes, the lender sells them in denominations of $5,000 to individual investors or to other institutions (usually securities dealers) who resell them to their clients. Sometimes a lender will simply place the MBS in its mutual mortgage fund portfolio.

"Cannie Maes" come in two forms: initially the underlying mortgages were from private homeowners, who were entitled to pay off the mortgages before the securities matured. In this type of Cannie Mae, your current yield will vary as the borrowers make prepayments. Mortgages may also go into default and mature. As these events occur, your cash flow will more and more consist of principal amortization rather than interest. On the other hand, you may benefit if prepayments are accompanied by penalties.

In August 1988, CMHC expanded the MBS program to include social housing mortgages. Since these mortgages *cannot* be prepaid, the yield on social MBS is fixed for their term. They have been understandably successful in the market. In the first year following their introduction, there were 90 issues totalling $649.1 million.

By autumn 1992, there were approximately 1,000 outstanding issues totalling $12 billion of all types of Cannie Maes issued by financial institutions across Canada. Because they're government insured, Cannie Maes are secure and widely available. Yields are generally in line with GIC rates and about 40 to 60 basis points (four- to six-tenths of a percentage point) above similar length Government of Canada bonds.

But if the rates are generally in line with GICs, why buy Cannie Maes instead of GICs? Promoters cite the following: there's no limit to the NHA guarantee on its MBS versus the $60,000 deposit insurance with GICs from an institutional lender; the stronger NHA guarantee of timely payment compared with that of the private institution; a preference by some investors for the monthly payout on the Cannie Maes; and, finally, the existence of an active secondary market in Cannie Maes.

If you buy MBS on the secondary market, your current yield will vary according to market interest rates. For instance, if market interest rates decline and you buy the MBS above par, your yield to maturity will be lower than the current yield. And, of course, the converse applies if market interest rates have increased and you can buy MBS at a discount.[61] When you sell MBS, you may experience capital gains or losses.

Ironically, even with no change in market interest rates, you can usually get yields of 1/4%-1/2% higher if you buy Cannie Maes on the secondary market, instead of when they're initially issued. As one leading mortgage banker notes, Cannie Maes are a "commission driven product that has been basically sold to unsophisticated retail accounts." So the higher yield on the secondary market (created by the lower price you'll pay for them) better reflects their value.

Mutual Mortgage Funds

Mutual mortgage funds allow you to participate in a much wider variety of mortgages than does the MBS. The funds are open-ended and the mortgages are constantly changing as old ones come due and are discharged or renewed and new ones are originated.

However, mutual mortgage funds offer no guarantees as to principal and interest payment. And because the mortgages themselves are not consistent in the length of term and interest rate, your return will vary.

The largest mutual mortgage fund, Royal Trust's M Fund, had a year end 1991 portfolio of 11,627 residential first mortgages with a market value of $964 million; 13.4% of that value was insured, its one year rate of return to unit holders was 20.7%; five years, 9.8%; 10 years 13.7%.

Before putting your money into third-party control for the purchase of mortgages, you should know exactly what's going on. Legal registration with a provincial authority is no guarantee of anything.

A spectacular illustration of mortgage investing gone wrong came to light in 1992 when Ontario seized the mortgage broker's licence and froze the assets of Holden Financial Corporation. Holden, a nine-branch company headed by dynamic seminar giver David Holden, had taken in $9.7 million in investments from several hundred investors who thought they were sharing in a pool of specific first and second mortgages. Instead, according to the government-appointed trustee, much of the money had simply been transferred into Holden's general accounts. And what mortgage investments did exist bore no relationship to any of the individual investors; some were assigned mortgages, others not, all on a totally arbitrary basis. As we go to press, the court was deciding whether all or only some of the investors should get a share of what was left and the government was investigating whether the collapse is grounds for prosecution.

CHAPTER 29

Syndications and MURBs

Syndications

Have you ever thought how satisfying it might be to own a shopping center, or an office tower, a hotel or quality apartment building? Yet you have only a fraction of the funds and none of the expertise necessary to do so? If so, real estate syndication may be just what you're looking for.

In a syndication, a number of investors pool their funds. Then the money is invested by the syndicate manager or promoter, who selects the property or properties and handles the entire investment process.

Defined broadly, syndications take several basic forms: limited partnerships, mutual funds, joint ventures and trusts. Whatever the form, syndicates buy or build virtually every type of property — from hotels to office buildings, shopping centers, industrial parks, public mini warehousing, apartment buildings and even single family homes. Though they're rare today, syndicates can also be formed to buy vacant land for future capital appreciation and development.

By combining their resources, small real estate investors can obtain the financial clout required to get prime properties that, individually, would be beyond their reach. Pooling funds enables you to buy the expert legal, accounting, construction, management and leasing talent needed for a successful investment. And it means you can be both a small and passive investor in a specific piece of quality, leveraged real estate.

Syndications can also help you diversify your holdings, so that you can invest outside your community, province or even outside the country.

Probably the most common form syndication takes today is the limited partnership. You usually become a limited partner by purchasing limited partnership units in projects under construction or already completed. However, the actual management is in the hands of the general partner (the promoter) or a subsidiary with broad powers.

The promoter usually wears several hats — such as general partner, developer, manager. There's nothing nefarious about this, as long as there's full disclosure. But this multiplicity of function under various corporate guises does pose possible conflicts of interest. For instance, the general partner could be buying services and materials on behalf of the limited partnership. But the company it's buying them from is often just the promoter sporting another corporate face.

As a limited partner, your management rights are restricted to certain major decisions, such as approving or rejecting the sale or exchange of the property, dissolving the partnership, or removing the general partner if it's in default of its obligations under the agreement. However, you are usually entitled to any distributable cash flow from the property rentals and any proceeds from the sale or refinancing of the project.

The general partner profits through the following:

Fixed Administrative and Managerial Fees
These can take on an almost infinite variety of forms, limited in many cases only by the promoter's ingenuity. In one publicly-traded setup, for instance, the general partner of a property fund receives an *acquisition fee* equal to 1.5% of the cost of each property bought. It also gets a yearly fee equal to 1% of the equity for *accounting services, a 5% property management fee* and a 1% *disposition fee.* Other such charges include *management* and *marketing fees, cash flow guarantee fees* and *basic management fees.*

Contracting and General Development Fees
The general partner grants itself certain fees to be earned for providing such services and commitments as interim financing, cash flow and mortgage guarantees, leasing services and building appraisal, and whatever other items it chooses to include in the agreement. These bits and pieces can add up to substantial returns for the promoter, which often has little of its own money at stake outside the initial cost of selling the units.

A "Carried Interest" in the Project
The promoter almost always gives itself a right to a percentage of the distributions and proceeds. In one partnership, for instance, the general partner received 7.5% of the net income (after a certain minimum amount was paid to the limited partners) and 15% of gains on properties the partnership sold.

Selling Assets to the Partnership
Often all or part of the real estate that is to be owned by the limited partnership is sold to it by the promoter. These assets may be sold at a cost determined by the promoter's own valuators, who may or may not be certified appraisers.

As a result of the corporate registration of the partnership, your liability as a limited partner is ordinarily limited to the amount of your subscription. But this can be lost if the general partner doesn't file and maintain the proper papers with regulatory authorities. Also, depending on the agreement, you may be called upon for further contributions.

The investment risks you face are primarily those facing any developer or purchaser of investment real estate. The project may be poorly constructed, located or managed — or any combination thereof. And, of course, it will be subject to market competition. The office market is particularly prone to a boom-bust cycle. Shopping centers always face the threat of newer competitors and a recessionary economy that could cut retail sales and consequently the percentage rents you would derive.

Investing in industrial or warehouse space is risky, too. Competitors can throw up new buildings in less than a year; economic recession will reduce the demand for space and maybe even drive your own tenants out of business altogether. Some cities have carried rent-depressing, industrial surpluses for as many as five years.

You also face the special risk of syndications: buying overpriced property and services from promoters with more experience as securities salesmen than real estate developers. This is especially true of syndications offering extensive tax sheltering features. In their zest to avoid taxes, investors may overlook the offering's shaky real estate fundamentals.

In return for the risks, what are the rewards you can reasonably expect? And how do they differ from holding shares in a public real estate company?

As with any real estate investment, the tangible benefits are cash flow from operations, capital appreciation, tax benefits and equity build-up.

As well, you benefit from the leverage of mortgage financing. The financed portion of most projects tends to be 30% to 50% of the total. These ratios are kept relatively low because of the experiences with high interest rates that bankrupted many syndicated real estate investments in the early '80s.

The cash flow from operations is the cash you get back each year on your initial investment after debt servicing and operating expenses, but before taxes. As a broad rule, this return rarely equals the return you'd get on a fixed-interest institutional deposit.

The *chief attraction is long-term appreciation of the property*, although as rents rise over the years, cash flow should increase too.

Tax benefits also help offset initially low-cash-on-cash returns. The most significant tax benefit left is capital cost allowance (also known as depreciation) which permits the reduction of the property's income but is not a cash cost. But this depreciation is recaptured and taxed when the property is resold. Also, if you borrowed money to buy your partnership units, you may be able to deduct the interest from taxable income. But if there is no such tax benefit, it's probably best not to borrow.

Compared to public real estate stocks, the value of syndication units is likely to be more stable. Like real estate stocks, they will sell well below the breakup value of the underlying real estate. The biggest difference, though, is that virtually all income from syndication units must be distributed to the unit holders (limited partners). In a public company there's little likelihood of that ever happening.

However, unlike shares in public companies or solely-owned real estate, most syndications offer only limited liquidity. *There's usually no regular market for selling or exchanging your interest in the partnership.*

Though some promoters offer limited buy-back privileges, these are usually exercisable only in extreme cases. Typically, you have to go bankrupt or die. Units managed by well-known general partners change hands more frequently, and sometimes even at a premium. But as a general rule, you shouldn't count on liquidating your investment for at least five to seven years. Also, you cannot usually pledge your units as collateral for loans. If you buy into a syndication, count on being in for the duration, like it or not. Consequently, the money you put in a syndicate shouldn't be money that you need to live on.

Syndications come in all shapes and sizes. And each province has its own lengthy definitions and restrictions. Ontario, for instance, requires universal registration of all securities issuers. "Private" syndications, which usually have no more than 25 participants and must not be offered to more than 50 potential investors, aren't required to file a prospectus or issue financial statements. However, an "offering memorandum" may be reacquired Because of the limited number of partners and to avoid the cost and complications of issuing a prospectus, private syndication units tend to cost more than public ones — usually a minimum of $150,000 versus $10,000 or so for many public offerings.

Public syndications appeal to a larger number of investors and are generally required by securities commissions to file a prospectus and financial statements. There's no evidence though that public syndications are any more or less successful than private ones.

Prospectuses give you much of the information you need to intelligently evaluate the partnership. But they "don't really summarize in any way exactly what's going on," says an investment and syndications expert with Royal LePage Ltd. "You have to go through the whole thing and figure out what you're paying and what you're getting."

Before getting involved in a syndication — either public or private — you should ask the following questions:

What is the promoter's track record? Who are the individuals behind it? In the case of a small private syndication, you should check out bank or business references. If the promoter has done previous projects, how well have they done? Speak to investors in other syndications the promoter has created.

Even if the promoter claims it is a private syndication, check out its status with provincial officials. In a recent Ontario securities fraud, the promoter continued to sell units in real estate projects despite a cease-trade order and court-ordered asset freeze. Between 1987 and 1990 the Consortium Group of Companies reeled in more than 500 investors to contribute $7.5 million for co-ownership projects. According to the Ontario Securities Commission, the brochures used to sell partnership units were full of misrepresentations and every single project was in difficulty from either a legal or financial perspective.[64]

What's the promoter's retained interest? It's usually a plus that the promoter has an interest in the project. But how much are you giving away for that interest? And if you're at risk, are you the only one? What can the promoter suffer?

Is the real estate you're buying sensibly priced and well located? What is the competition like — both present and future? And what is the demand for the property? The tax shelter is usually shallow, so the real estate must stand on its own.

What incentives does the promoter have for finishing new projects on time and managing them successfully?

What are the guarantees in the package? And what are they worth? For instance, if there's a guarantee of x return, how is it guaranteed? by the promoter's covenant? a bank credit line? "You might ask yourself, too, " says Gamble, "that if a guarantee is really necessary, should you be investing in the deal at all?"

In small private deals, who are your co-investors? Are they prepared for the long haul? Can they afford further funds if they're needed? Equally important, can you afford further contributions?

What will be the tax effects of the investment? Because these vary enormously depending on individual circumstances, you should get your own tax adviser's opinion. Don't rely on the promoter's opinion. And don't forget to include the cost of this advice in calculating your projected return. Also, keep in mind that certain deductions and allowances may be challenged at any time by Revenue Canada, and that the department will not give advance tax rulings on limited partnerships.

How realistic are the promoter's projections? To help you evaluate the various syndicated projects, promoters' prospectuses include pro formas that extend ten to 15 years into the future. These predict such things as income, disbursements, debt service, distributable cash and the tax effects at various marginal tax rates.

They are interesting documents, well worth looking at. But remember that detailed pro formas are only as good as the assumptions underlying them. So how realistic are they? All projections are subject to the quality of the project, its management, market competition at the time of completion and the future state of the economy.

It's one thing to project steadily rising rental rates and occupancy levels. It may be quite another thing to reach them.

In hotels, for instance, says Gamble, "the trick is to sell the project on the basis of a higher room rate than reality indicates and then use the investor's money to subsidize the rents."

Invariably, too, all pro formas reflect the universal optimism of real estate developers.

American developer Kimball W. Small, president of Kimball Small Properties, puts it succinctly: "[Developers] are like drug addicts. All we need is money. If you keep shoving it at us, we'll build."

Finally, remember to consider your opportunity costs, says Gamble. That's what most people miss out on. Do you really want a piece of a hotel? an apartment building? an office tower? Maybe it's not your best investment. There are always alternatives.

Here's how one public syndication is set up. It's an offering of limited partnership units in a 300-room downtown hotel yet to be built. To make it attractive to the smallest of investors, units cost just $12,500. You only have to pay $1,500 on subscription. You pay the balance over four years in installments every six months of $2,000, $2,000, $1,500, $1,500, and four payments of $1,000 each, plus accrued interest. Each $12,500-unit supports another $28,294 in nonrecourse mortgage financing and the "carried" interest of the promoter.

The total price to the investing public is $4.83 million; the agent selling the securities gets $338,000, leaving net proceeds of about $4.5 million.

Besides this equity, the project is financed with two mortgages totalling $10.1 million: a first for $9.1 million at an estimated annual rate of 11.65% per annum calculated semi-annually, amortized for 35 years with a five-year term; and a second for $1 million for five years at 14% annual interest, prepaid and included in the development costs. This is a mortgage back to the promoter as partial payment for the land that it's selling to the limited partnership.

The total cost — the amount paid by the limited partnership to acquire and complete the hotel — is $15.8 million.

The promoter gets a 40% interest in the limited partnership by selling the land for $4.5 million. The stated capital for this contribution is $850,000. (By contrast, the other limited partners are paying $4.84 million for their 60% of the equity.) As well, the promoter is taking back a second mortgage for $1 million and is receiving $2.65 million in cash.

At its option, the promoter can convert its vendor-take-back second mortgage into a further 10% equity interest. If not converted, the second mortgage becomes a participating second mortgage renewable for two five-year terms with debt service equal to 162/3% of "available cash for distribution" to the limited partners. (Available cash for distribution is essentially gross revenues after operating expenses, debt service, reserves and various incentive fees to the manager.)

Once completed, the hotel will be managed by an arm's-length hotel management company under a renewable 20-year agreement.

The manager will receive a basic management fee of 3.5% of gross revenues, an unspecified group services fee for such items as group advertising, promotion and reservations and an incentive management fee equal to 10% of the gross operating profit. In addition, the manager is to get up to 75% of available cash for distribution after certain payments to the limited partners. It is also to get 20% of any consideration in excess of $17.5 million that the limited partnership gets from disposing of the hotel.

Besides its 40% carried interest — which it may increase to 50% — the project's promoter stands to benefit through a number of fees and profits for various services, including:

- underlying mortgage placement fee of $91,000 for arranging a first mortgage on the hotel;
- mortgage indemnification fee of $136,500 for assuming the liabilities for principal and interest payments under the first mortgage;
- construction and services fees of $585,500, of which approximately $159,250 is said to be profit.

The promoter, in its capacity as a developer, says it is doing the actual development and construction of the hotel on a nonprofit basis for $10.6 million. So what are the benefits to you as the investor?

For the first five years of hotel operation you get a 7% annual return of equity guaranteed by the promoter; and you could also get up to 20% of available cash for distribution.

You also get a proportionate interest in any profit on disposition of the hotel or any refinancing proceeds in excess of those necessary to discharge other debt or maintain the property.

For taxpayers in the 50% tax bracket, there are also substantial tax savings. Thanks to capital cost allowance and soft cost deductions, after five years each unit is projected to have generated a tax loss of $6,346 while, in fact, having generated a cash flow of $5,727. (Since this project, tax laws have been changed to preclude you from creating or increasing a loss from a hotel operation.)

As a limited partner, you naturally have no say whatsoever in the hotel's development. However, you may be called upon for additional capital contributions by a 75% vote of the limited partners.

You can redeem your units from the partnership under a complicated formula based on the amount of available cash for distribution in the year you want. If you die, your estate has a right to redeem within a year of your death, though there will be some major deductions.

MURBs

The federal MURB program (short for Multiple Unit Residential Building) was devised in the mid-70s as a way to encourage the development of rental housing. Investors in MURB projects were allowed to use certain "soft" development costs as well as capital cost allowance to reduce their taxable income from other sources. Normally, you can only use such deductions to reduce revenues from the real estate itself to zero.

The MURB program expired in 1981, but until the 1987 Income Tax Reform, all existing MURBs remained MURBs until they were demolished. So after the original MURB owner had exhausted all the tax benefits, a new MURB investor could buy the unit and start over again. Although the transaction could be arranged between individual MURB owners, what often happened was that a syndicator would buy an entire MURB project, then "repackage" and resell the units. However, the 1987 reform put an end to this practice. The only exception is for any MURB project registered with a public authority *prior* to June 18, 1987, the date the reforms were first made public. And regardless of when you buy the MURB, you can take advantage of writeoffs in all tax years before the 1994 tax year. After 1994, there'll be a rush of MURB has-beens onto the market, predicts Royal LePage commercial real estate fund manager, Morris Mostowyk.

MURBs can be structured in two ways: 1) as limited partnership MURBs, wherein you own a portion of the partnership which, in turn, owns the MURB; or 2) as individually titled units, which you own outright, and can sell and manage as you see fit.

Though you could own an entire MURB building yourself, most of these individually titled MURBs are condominium units — either high-rise apartments or townhouses. Of the two forms of ownership, the limited partnership obviously offers less flexibility to the owner. Furthermore, as a limited partner, there are more restrictions on losses you can take for a particular taxation year than if you were an outright owner. Here's how one recent MURB sale was set up:

The promoter offered 202 individually-titled condominium apartments in a 15-storey tower in the suburbs of a large city. The building was built in 1979 and the MURB benefits to the original owners had expired. The promoter acquired all the suites from the original investors, then packaged and promoted their sale to new investors. In this offering, you paid $75,000 for a 1,000-square-foot, two-bedroom unit, and $82,000 for a 1,200-square-foot three-bedroom unit.

The financing set up by the developer — and on which its projections are based — required only a $1,000 down payment on your part; the balance of the purchase price was financed by mortgages and bank loans set up by the promoter. For the two-bedroom unit, there was a $15,000 floating rate bank loan, and an institutional first and a VTB second mortgage totalling $59,000 amortized for 30 years coming due in five years at a blended rate not exceeding 10.875%, the three-bedroom unit was similarly financed.

The promoter undertook to manage the property for five years and provide a cash flow deficiency guarantee for any shortfall beyond that stated in its six-year pro-forma. The deficiency guarantee cost $6,000, plus there was an "initial services and interim operations fee" of $2,200. However, both these fees were optional.

Presume you paid those fees and that your marginal tax rate was 55.5% in 1986 and 52.5% for the balance.

Then, according to the promoter, buying a two-bedroom unit would give you a total tax savings over six years of $22,851 and a cumulative cash surplus of $2,840. Assuming the building goes up 4% a year in value, your net proceeds on sale would be $14,473; and your after tax gains on sale, including the cost of disposing of your unit, would be $8,077. Certainly a very impressive gain on your $1,000 investment the equivalent of earning 56% annually on that $1,000 investment.

Although this type of MURB sale is much simpler than most syndications, you still have to consider many questions. How realistic are the promoter's projections? Are there adequate provisions made for maintenance and repair? Will rents increase as much as it claims? Will the property rise in value to the extent it projects?

Nothing beats taking a look at the property and the neighborhood. Is it in a declining neighborhood? Or is it a rising one?

If you choose to pay for any "guarantee," how reliable is that guarantee? Is it just the developer's promise or are there funds placed out of its control to fund any deficiency?

If you're not in the top marginal tax bracket, does the investment make sense? Why buy tax shelters if you don't have income to shelter.

CHAPTER 30

Landlord-Tenant Relations

One thing that many real estate investors overlook is the simple fact that it's not the properties themselves that generate their day-to-day cash flow — it's their tenants' rent that keeps them going until the property is sold.

Selecting good tenants and staying on reasonable terms with them is therefore a key ingredient in successful real estate investing. It requires time, effort and preparation. Overlook it and you can turn a sweet investment sour.

Tenants are the least controllable element in your investment calculations. Just one mistake can throw your most carefully laid plans into disarray. Tenants are truly the key to success in long-term rental properties. In fact, good tenant relations should start even before you buy the building. That's because the kind of building you purchase — its location, condition, the size of the suites, the number of bedrooms and amenities — will determine the kinds of tenants you'll attract.

Buy close to a university and you'll attract students. Buy a building that's mostly three-bedroom apartments and you will attract families. Buy a rundown building and you'll get tenants to match.

Although usually the type of tenants applying to rent is predetermined by the building, this isn't always the case. Some buildings can go any one of several ways. The danger in such a building is that you'll be tempted to mix incompatible groups. Families with children may be used to screaming kids running down the halls. But don't expect retirees to exhibit the same tolerance. In any case, it's best to stick with the class of people that present you with the fewest management headaches.

At the top of the heap, are the so-called "empty nesters" — married couples who have moved out of home because their children have grown. They tend to live quietly, pay promptly and take good care of the premises.

176

Another desirable group of tenants is career people — whether single or married. They like smaller units in well-established areas and are not inclined to throw wild parties.

Families with children are a big part of the rental market. But with children in an apartment building, you can figure on repairs and maintenance costs being at least double what they would otherwise be.

At the bottom of the heap come young adult males. They're often noisy, demanding and quick to complain. Also, newly cohabiting couples tend to have little regard for other occupants of a building, and they may leave at a moment's notice when their relationship breaks up.

Students are in a category by themselves. They tend to be either very good or very bad. Some landlords swear by them; others swear at them. The general rule for students is to rent only to mixed groups of men and women or women only; and if possible to rent to graduate rather than undergraduate students. Also, get firm letters of guaranty from parents or other working adults who live nearby, so that they can be held responsible in the event of non-payment of rent.

When you're selecting tenants, the safest attitude to have — though not to express — is that your property is under attack by vandals who want to live in it rent free and demand your time and money for the privilege of allowing them to do so.

Never forget: As a property owner you're not in the social services department; you're not a charity; you're not a public utility. You have no obligation to house anyone you don't want to — though, of course, you cannot legally discriminate against anyone on the basis of race, creed, religion, national origin and, in some jurisdictions, age and sexual orientation.

Never forget: It's your property — your $20,000 or $50,000 or $200,000 asset — that they'll be using. It's amazing how many small investors won't lend the family car to their children for a night without a stern recitation of rules and restrictions, then turn around and surrender possession of a $150,000 home to a stranger after a ten-minute, unsubstantiated chat.

Your first line of defence against undesirables — is the written application. Surprisingly, most small landlords ignore this elementary device; they just take the first applicant with money and a convincing smile.

Unfortunately this is not enough. One investor we know found this out when he rented his house to a demure young lady and her fiancé, whom the investor did not meet. The fiancé turned out to be a member of a motorcycle club and the investor's house became the club's headquarters.

People who are poor, ignorant, criminal or violent aren't necessarily stupid. And especially so when it comes to dealing with naive middle-class landlords. "Professional" deadbeats make a career of renting from small landlords. They can easily move from place to place and live rent free. When one landlord evicts them, they simply move on to another place. Count on taking at least six months to legally evict such a tenant for nonpayment of rent. Such people are also likely to be judgment-proof.

Your rental application form should ask for the applicant's full name and social insurance number, plus information on:

- the applicant's current and *previous* landlords
- rent and length of tenancies
- current employment, including salary, position and length of time employed
- names of spouse, children and all other people who will live on the premises, along with their ages and relationships to one another
- full credit and banking references and all outstanding loans and monthly payments
- make and year of automobile and licence number; and the applicant's driver's licence number. If the car is a late model, there could be hefty payments on it, which could cut into the applicant's ability to pay your rent.

Request references, too. Anyone who can't give the names of three people who know them may not have much stability.

Finally, be sure to ask for the names of people to notify in case of emergency — in case the tenant becomes seriously sick, injured or dies on the premises.

To comply with consumer protection legislation, your application should have a clause in which prospective tenants give you the right to check their credit.

Along with the application, applicants should fill out, sign and seal an *offer to lease*. As the name implies, the offer is the tenant's formal written request to you that he wishes to lease the premises on the terms that are spelled out in the offer.

Along with the offer, you should get rent for at least one month in advance as a sign of good faith on the applicant's part. If the payment is by cheque, get it certified or cash it; that way, you've tested the applicant's seriousness. If you accept his offer within the time period stipulated, and he changes his mind, the deposit is forfeited and you can sue him for further damages. Naturally, if you don't accept the offer, you must immediately refund the deposit.

Experienced landlords are often leery of cash rental deposits. Why doesn't the applicant have a chequing account? Sure, the sight of money is impressive. And the applicant knows it. But that rent for the first and last month may be the only money you'll ever see from him.

Checking the applicant's current landlord is not all that useful. Even if they're dreadful tenants, the landlord will be inclined to give a good recommendation to get rid of them. Therefore, the landlord prior to the current one is more likely to give a realistic assessment.

In any case, an undesirable applicant may well not tell you where he's really living. Instead, he gives the names and addresses of relatives or friends. Or some story about staying only at a "temporary" residence. Or that he's moving in from "out of town."

To help you smoke out the truth, you can ask your bank manager to check the applicant's credit through either contacting their bank or tapping into the local credit bureau. There may be a fee for this service, and bankers may not give you the details of their inquiries. But they will tell you whether the report is negative or not.

In some areas, too, there are private services that keep track of landlord/tenant actions in local courts. These are helpful in picking up on applicants who have slipped through your credit and employment checks.

In case you still have any doubts about an applicant, dropping by their current residence can help set your mind at rest. Obviously, this is only practicable for the small landlord with just a few rental units.

You have no obligation to tell applicants why you turned them down. And the less you do say, the better. Choosing the proper tenants takes you halfway to your goal of profitable property management. Going the rest of the way requires a mixture of common sense, knowledge of landlord-tenant law and a thick skin.

The obligations and rights of landlords, tenants and third parties in landlord-tenant relations and their formal documentation differ across the country. And they are voluminous. Ontario's residential tenancies and rent control acts alone occupy 150 pages. So we can't begin to summarize them here. The only way you can be somewhat sure of what rules prevail where you live is to obtain the latest copy of your provincial landlord and tenant and rent control acts and regulations.

We say "somewhat sure" for two reasons: 1) sometimes, as in Ontario last year, new rent control legislation can be held up for more than a year while politicians wrangle and wangle for votes; and 2) the broad powers bestowed on the rental tribunals, with their penchant for "people's courts," renders any projections of the effect of a law problematic.[65] Don't expect sympathy or understanding from your tenants. And certainly don't mistake them for friends.

Whether you are renting on a weekly, monthly or year-to-year basis, you should have a well-drafted lease. This is mainly for your own protection, since tenants are already well-protected by legislation. The lease should eliminate any ambiguities as to the rights and responsibilities of both sides to the contract.

Rules against pets are a contentious issue. Even if you have rules against them, tenants will inevitably slip them in. And once they're in, in many jurisdictions, they're not grounds for eviction. (A condominium is a different case.)

In practice, whether pets are a problem or not depends on the tenant. Quiet clean people generally have quiet clean pets. The most contentious animals walk on two legs.

Generally, in residential leases you can't "contract out" of the law. You and your tenant can mutually agree to a host of things — ranging from rent levels to rights of access. But if it violates the law, it's irrelevant and unenforceable. As mentioned earlier, provincial requirements differ. For instance:

- In Ontario, if you don't deliver a copy of the lease to your residential tenants within 21 days from the start of their tenancy, they don't have to pay you rent until they receive the lease. Then all arrears will have to be paid.
- In Quebec, upon signing a lease or concluding a verbal lease, the landlord must give the tenant a notice stating the lowest amount of rent paid during the 12-month period preceding the beginning of the lease, or the amount of rent fixed by the Regie du lodgement. But no matter what rent you mutually agree to, the tenant can appeal it to the Regie within ten days and the Regie may roll it back.
- In Ontario, the landlord is also required to give new tenants written notice of the maximum rent. Plus: the date of the most recent increase, any pending application under the act, any current order and any notice of pending appeal. As well, the tenant has two years to dispute the legality of the rent.
- In Ontario, there is no formal mechanism for the withholding of rent when the landlord is in breach of his obligations.[66] But in Quebec, rent may by law be deposited with the Regie.

When you give the tenants possession of the rental unit, you should mutually fill in an inspection report, noting any damage to such things as windows, doors and appliances. This provides both parties with evidence of the condition of the premises at the start of the lease in case there's a dispute when the tenants leave.

The billing of utilities is another crucial matter in a small rental property. Many a small landlord renting out his or her first house is amazed to find that utilities cost at least double those for an owner-occupied home. The temperature stays a toasty 23°C in the winter — with a window or two opened for continuous fresh air. Lights, televisions and auxiliary beaters are used indiscriminately. It's only logical behaviour, though. If it's free, why conserve it?

Of course, as a practical matter, in an apartment house, unmetered utilities can only be borne by the landlord. But if you're renting, say a converted home with two-four units, the absence of separate metering shouldn't preclude separate billing.

When tenants move in, have the lease provide that they will be responsible for x% of the entire property's utility bills. You can provide for paying these bills in three ways: a) one tenant can be totally responsible for them, including collecting the other tenants' portions; b) you can pay the bills as they come in and then charge the tenants back their agreed-upon share — which will leave you shelling out while they take their time in repaying you; or c) you can "equal bill" your tenants an amount estimated as the monthly average of one year worth of utility costs. Then you can periodically adjust that estimate with the actual costs.

Generosity with appliances can cost you dearly. One property owner recounts how she provides not only free washers and dryers, but pays for the electricity and hot water as well. Her tenants have responded by taking in all their friends' washing too. In the tight rental market in many cities today, it's often unnecessary to supply stoves and fridges, let alone dishwashers, washers and dryers. Luxury units are an exception.

Assuming you've avoided these two contentious pitfalls — and assuming you've chosen responsible tenants — any subsequent breakdown in good relations can often be traced to poor communications.

When people don't know why something is happening — or not happening — they get understandably irritated. So if repairs are being made to a boiler that will necessitate shutting it off, let the tenants know beforehand.

Fix small things quickly. And, if major repairs are needed, let tenants know it and let them know how soon you expect them to be completed. People who have never owned property or dealt with tradespeople have little notion of the time that can be involved — of the tradesmen who don't show up, who drag jobs out and who fail to start or complete the task when they say they will. So make sure you always allow a lot of extra time for these inevitable delays.

Bear in mind that your aim is to keep good tenants for as long as you can. Even in a tight rental market, there are substantial costs involved when tenants move — advertising, showing prospects the property, checking their credit and so on. As well, an empty apartment or house emphasizes all the flaws that furnishings hide. So you may have to redecorate to attract new tenants.

Smooth landlord-tenant relationships can keep good tenants on at lease renewal time. Make concessions if necessary. If tenants ask if you will paint if they renew, don't stubbornly refuse unless you're sure they'll stay anyway. Surprisingly, some landlords won't paint for an existing tenant. But they will turn around and redecorate to re-rent the apartment to new tenants.

If you're concerned about losing good tenants because you have to raise the rent, you could modify your increase to some extent. After all, a vacant unit costs money. Any increase you could have gotten may be wiped out by the costs of keeping the unit vacant. Empty apartments don't bring in any rents.

Alternatively, you might offer free improvements — carpeting, say, or a new appliance. Besides having the tenant for another year or so, these improvements may enhance the rental or sale value of the property when the tenant eventually does move on.

Although dealing with tenants and with the property is essential, there is one other consideration to keep in mind as your assets and your responsibilities accumulate: amidst the whirl of renovating, renting and refinancing, you must make sure you don't overlook the importance of good record-keeping.

Many landlords do. Worse still, they start keeping records in their heads. Or they jot them down in such a cryptic manner that soon they forget what they mean. In no time, you can weave an impenetrable jungle. You can lose control over your own investment — miss tax deductions, overstate income and understate losses. It's disconcertingly easy to lose count of whether rent is paid or not. You can tell the tenant you have no record of payment. But if you don't have any record of any payments, how will you prove your case even if you take him to court? Disentangling the mess can take many times longer than doing it right in the first place.

Record keeping is not your most important job as an owner-manager. But without proper records, you won't know whether you're making money or losing it in a dozen different ways. Good records can help you spot:

- expenses that are getting out of line
- reasons for lasting vacancies
- how long it takes to fill those vacancies
- which of your units are most easily rented
- what types of tenants are the most desirable
- theft or waste by any managers or others you employ

And, most importantly, without full records you'll be hard put to justify rent increases.

An accountant or bookkeeper using standard business forms can help you devise the precise kinds of records you will need. Essentially, the records you maintain should enable you to keep tabs on *income, expenses and taxes*. The basic records you'll need to account for include:

- a rental schedule
- rent receipts
- bank deposit slips
- rent collection records
- monthly rental summary
- record of deposits

For expenses, you will need:

- a summary of disbursements
- a cheque register
- monthly vacancy reports and, if your property is large
- monthly operating statements

Records that are not immediately relevant need not be kept. Old rental or employee applications, for example, can be safely thrown out after a year. But any document relating to the purchase, sale or exchange of property, capital improvements or costs should be kept indefinitely, although not necessarily at hand. If you sell a building 40 years from today, Revenue Canada may demand the information to determine your tax liability.

CHAPTER 31

No Money Down

The crowd files in, taking every chair as directed by the ushers. All eyes focus forward as the speaker bounds to the front, his three-piece blue suit perfectly creased.

"Hi!"

"Hi!" the audience yells back.

Then, with a hillbilly twang reminiscent of the battling banjoes in *Deliverance*, the speaker races along: "Are *you* ready to change *your* life? All you need is a good positive need and a will to make money. We're going to show *you* how *you* can buy real estate, faster, quicker and safer than you ever have before; how *you* can create financial independence in five years in just *one* weekend a month."

The style is part television evangelist, part CNE barker, part SCTV parody come to life.

The nattily attired pitchman, and his brothers in hyperbole, are a familiar sight in the hotel ballrooms of southern Ontario, Alberta, Vancouver and Montreal. And on the late night TV screen.

Flip your TV dial around midnight and, depending on the state of the real estate market, odds are you'll see one of a number of late night/early morning "no money down" hustlers: squeaky-voiced Ed Beckley, self-styled "Millionaire Maker"; Tom Vu, a Vietnamese refugee turned Orlando, Florida, "Profit, Profit, Profit" preacher who does most of his deep thinking, his ads suggest, cruising the south Florida canal system in a crush of busty babes; fast talking Dave Del Dotto and his "Cash Flow System"; and relatively flashless Canadians Albert Lowery and Raymond Aron.

Although their allure has been considerably tarnished by lawsuits and consent orders in the cases of Raymond Vu and Ed Beckley, late night real estate "informercials" still pop up between the depilatory testimonials and juice machine hucksters. While their shows are 100% advertising, the promoters are charged only 12 minutes an hour of advertising, the maximum permitted by the CRTC. Each one promises to reveal the secrets of success in real estate. No job? No cash? No credit? No problem. All you need to do is follow your favorite leader's simple directions to financial independence via real estate investment.

The "powerful money-making ideas" in his course show you how to make $3,000 a month in 90 days after you complete it, Beckley promises.

Partly the courses teach techniques — no money down formulas, negotiating tactics, credit creation. But, as important, they preach attitude. Sometimes consciously, sometimes not, they freely borrow the ideas of every positive-thinking, self-actualizing guru from Napoleon Hill to Wayne Dyer. Beckley himself practices transcendental meditation several hours daily.

No-money down audiences are peppered with believers. Personal testaments abound.

"Is this a good deal?" one pitchman asks of his course. "It is! It is!" comes the reply. The converted bounce forward to give their stories of financial hopelessness turned to economic redemption thanks to the leader's instruction. "I started in July from zero. Now I control a half-million dollars in real estate. It has been fantastic !"

Praise the Lord and pass me my Mastercard!

You don't have to be "born again" to subscribe to the no-money-down gospel. Just be willing to pay for it. Beckley and Vu's employees and Aron himself (or employee Keith Watters) give two-hour teaser seminars, a quarter of which they devote to pitching the merits of signing up for the paid one- to two-day courses, which cost $495 to $695. Assorted books, home-study courses and tapes range from $99 to $395.

The promoters meet the shock of these charges with the L'Oreal hair coloring approach. It's not an expense. It's an "investment" in your future. Aren't *you* worth it?

"How much for all this [his course]?" Aaron asks himself. "I've been advised to charge $1,000. But the entire tuition is just $499. 'Mr. Aaron, that is amazing,' you say. 'But I don't have $499.' Well, if you don't have $499, you'd *better* take this course."

Beckley takes the amortization approach. "Isn't it worth 80 a day for a lifetime of financial independence? Invest in your future. May God bless you. And order now."

The hype is all pretty tempting. And certainly it's hard to argue with the importance of building a positive attitude. But many of the techniques the courses teach are questionable from a legal, practical and ethical standpoint, caution real estate experts.

"I think real estate is a great investment, a great way of building wealth, " says Toronto lawyer Alan Silverstein. "But I've got doubts about the way the no-down approach operates in Ontario.

"Number one, I think they're playing on the ignorance of vendors. And everyone realizes that. They're slanting everything against the interest of the vendor.

"And number two, there are some liabilities to the purchasers." Even if they aren't putting any money down, "they are making a commitment and they could find themselves in lawsuits if they do walk away from deals."

Whether you're a real estate salesperson or broker, or you're selling your home privately, you can't miss the impact of the no-money-down courses. The stereotyped approach and the absurd offers they urge their congregations to make are becoming a common nuisance, report real estate professionals.

"I get these people calling me all the time trying to buy a house for nothing down," says a successful real estate broker. "I tell them, 'I know where *you've* been. If you want to get serious, get a down payment together and I'll be happy to work with you.'"

Another homeowner put an ad in the paper for his own modest home. The first day alone he got 25 calls from no-money-down graduates. All were using variations of Ed Beckley's "Telephone Questionnaire," including the give-away question: "Why do you need cash?"

One approach to no-money-down buying that real estate experts find especially objectionable, though perfectly legal, is called the "Oklahoma Offer." Taught by Beckley and others, it involves "over mortgaging."

It works this way: the Beckleyite offers, say, on a $100,000 house — a $10,000 down payment, purchaser to arrange a new first of *at least* $60,000, vendor to take back a second mortgage of $30,000. Then the Beckleyite buyer arranges a first of *more* than $60,000, say $75,000. So not only is the Beckleyite not putting any money down, he can actually put money in his pocket on the closing. However, the vendor is left holding a VTB mortgage in excess of the value of the property. And the higher the first mortgage, the less safety there is for the vendor in case the buyer defaults. Institutional lenders normally won't touch this kind of deal.

"The customer should prove his good faith by having a down payment against the house," explains Richard Desrochers, assistant manager of personal lending and mortgages for the National Bank of Canada. "Otherwise, if he has problems with repairs or the like, he doesn't have even a dollar in it. So he has no interest in keeping the house."

Beckley also advocates subletting your way to riches — that is, find a property with a "below-market" rent, lease it and then sublet it for more to someone else. "You could create $1,000 to $1,500 income per month," he claims.

But you would also be liable for the rent on every lease. Besides, are there that many landlords who aren't already trying to get the highest rent they can and tenants trying to get the lowest rent? Finally, since all residential units are under rent control, how could you legally charge more than the landlord anyway? Besides showing you how to skirt the truth and skin unsuspecting vendors, no-money-down hustlers create "opportunities" out of whole cloth.

For example, a Beckley lecturer in Toronto says that bank-repossessed real estate is a good source of bargains. "We show you how to get that list in hand."

In reality, no lists are available to the public and even if they were they wouldn't be of much help. That's because, instead of using foreclosure, Canadian lenders much more often take over properties by a faster and cheaper procedure called "power of sale." And in power-of-sale proceedings, lenders are bound by law to make every effort to get top price for the property.

"If we drop the price to the mortgage outstanding, we as a bank are dead," says a Toronto Dominion Bank spokesman.

And a recent case illustrates what can happen when lenders neglect their duty. The lender, acting under the authority of its power of sale sold a hobby farm; in doing so, it ignored a valid offer the mortgagor had secured for $210,000. Instead, relying on negligent marketing and negligent appraisals, the trust company sold the property for $185,000. The mortgagor sued and the Court awarded him the $25,000 difference.[67]

While many of the no-money-down schemes wither under scrutiny, the proponents themselves have latched onto a good thing. And no one sums up their appeal better than Ed Beckley, who oversees a $30 million a year mail-order operation in Fairfield, Iowa.

"There's plenty of money in the world. People just lack ideas on how to attract that money. If you bundle incentives together, money will pursue those incentives. So all you need to do is package and create a situation where that money will flow in your direction."

It's long past time to reverse the flow — away from the hustlers and into sound real estate investments.

CHAPTER 32

Becoming an Agent

Chances are that if you've thought about investing in real estate, you've also toyed with the idea of becoming a real estate agent.

Popular myth to the contrary though, being an agent doesn't put you on the fast track to real estate investment riches. Certainly, there's big money to be made and you often don't have to know much about real estate to make it. But the super-agents with six-figure incomes are the exception.

Still, on the plus side, clearly agents have the opportunity of learning of local and office listings before nonlicensed buyers. Besides having access to the printed daily listings, increasing numbers of agents work directly off the listings entered into their local MLS computer system. But if you're in the hands of a good agent, you can find out about desirable properties just as fast. However, no matter how closely you work with your agent, you can't save much on commission costs.

But as an agent yourself, you'll normally earn commissions both when you buy and when you sell your property. So the price you pay is effectively lower than for a non-agent; and when you sell, the price you get is effectively higher than if you weren't an agent. If your commission split is favorable and/or you buy or sell your own listing, the savings can be substantial. For instance, in buying a $200,000 property, you could save up to $5,700 (if you're on a 95% split with your employing broker.)

Notwithstanding these benefits, in many ways it's a disadvantage being simultaneously agent and investor.

- You have to give up your anonymity and you can't keep any special information to yourself.
- Just because you're an agent, vendors may assume that you have special information, insight and intuition about the property and may stick stubbornly to their asking price.

188

- Both the common law of agency and provincial statutes strictly regulate the behavior of agents buying listed properties.

To begin with, you must, by law, inform the vendor, usually in writing, that you're an agent. This applies whether the property is listed with an agent or is being sold privately. In four provinces you must do so *before* you present your offer. In Manitoba, if you don't make disclosure, the vendor can rescind the transaction (cancel it and get his property back) up to 30 days after he discovers the true circumstances.[68]

At the same time, you must reveal all information you have pertaining to the current and future value of the property you're trying to buy. So if you know, say, that a developer may want to buy the property as part of an assembly for an apartment building, you must tell the vendor.

You also cannot make any secret negotiations or profits. So if you have a purchaser ready to take an assignment of the offer—in other words, you're planning a quick flip must disclose that. Even if you acquire an interest in a property *after* you've sold it—becoming a partner of the buyer, for instance—you could be in trouble if you sell it later for a profit.[69]

In short: unless you make full disclosure to the seller, you can't benefit financially in any way from the transaction.

If you're an agent in Manitoba, you cannot, by law, sue for your portion of a commission on a listed property that you buy, even where you've made full disclosure. Payment of the commission is totally voluntary on the part of the vendor. [70]

The province of New Brunswick goes further yet, compelling the agent to tell the owner to get independent advice regarding the real estate and its value.[71] Indeed, that may be prudent practice every time an agent is buying listed property.[72]

The courts have also strongly suggested that an agent buying listed property must notify the vendor that the agent/buyer will be receiving a portion of the commission.[73]

If you make an agreement to buy your own listing, the standard is higher yet. Even if the vendor refuses to close the transaction, "it is highly unlikely that the licensee will be successful in a specific performance action," says one authority. "There is a *very onerous* burden on the licensee to demonstrate that the transaction is a reasonable one as far as the vendor is concerned."[74] You can't evade the rules by having a friend or relative or company you control buy the property either. Some brokerage companies, such as Royal LePage, prohibit their agents from buying property for short-term speculation. If they violate this rule, they're fired.

Selling your own property is no easier.

Though the law doesn't always require you to tell the buyer you're an agent, Article 11 of the Standards of Business Practice of the Canadian Real Estate Association states that "in selling property owned by the Member, or in which he has an interest, his interest as known to the Member shall be revealed to the purchaser in writing."

A prospective buyer may think that if you're an agent selling your property, there must be something wrong with it. Perhaps you have some special information about a pending drop in the property's value. Otherwise, why would you be selling it? To avoid these questions on presenting their own offer, it's not unusual for real estate agents to buy and sell properties for themselves through other agents.

By contrast, if you're not an agent, what you know about the future value of the property is entirely your own business. You have a buyer in your "back pocket"? Fine. You have inside information that a developer needs the property to complete an assembly for a shopping center? Fine. Two hours after you sign the agreement of purchase and sale someone wants to pay you $10,000 to assign your offer. Fine. You know the property is priced $35,000 under market? Fine. (Though not so fine for the negligent agent who listed it that way!) As a nonlicensed buyer, the only interest you have to look after is your own.

Finally, if you're a real estate agent and you have any history of buying and selling property, you put yourself at risk of being viewed by Revenue Canada as a trader in real estate. Consequently, any gains you might make may be treated not as partially tax exempt capital gains, or even capital gains, but as ordinary fully taxable income.

Becoming a real estate agent can be an interesting and rewarding career. But it won't give you any magic pipeline to opportunities or riches as an investor.

Endnotes

1. Statistics Canada, 93-311, *Dwellings and Households, 1991 Census* (July 1992). The U.S. figure was 64.1%, U.S. Survey of income and Program Participation, 1984, as quoted in Statistics Canada, 75-001 E, vol.2, no 1., *The Distribution of Wealth in Canada and the United States*, Spring 1990.

2. Canadian Real Estate Association, *Annual Report, 1985; monthly report,* June 1992.

3. Statistics Canada, Table 9, Consumer Price Index for Canada All Items (Not Seasonally Adjusted), 1961-1985.

4. Toronto Real Estate Board, *House Price Trends and residential construction costs in the Toronto Real Estate Board Market Area,* (1985, 1992 Editions); MLS boundary changes in 1991 affect comparisons somewhat.

5. Canadian Real Estate Association, *Annual Report, 1985.*

6. Based on figures supplied by the Toronto Dominion Bank.

7. As the bankers will quickly point out, a comparison on the basis of buying the house for *all cash* works out in favour of the GICs. Investing $57,763 in GICS on April 18, 1975 and rolling the amount over each year would have given you a total of $159,226 by April 1985, $174,711 by 1986 and $189,877 by April 1987. But, by the same token, this return should be compared against the return from the *four* average homes you could have bought for your original $57,763. The four homes would have given you a gross gain of $426,596.

8. A.E. LePage (from 1985, Royal LePage) *Canadian Real Estate Surveys 1976-1989.*

9. *Ibid.,* Toronto Real Estate Board, *Insight 1992.*

10. But if your gross income is at least $45,000, even these otherwise tax free gains can still be taxed under the Alternative Minimum Tax (AMT). Under the AMT, one-half of the capital gains eligible for the exemption are taxed at a flat federal rate of 17%, plus provincial taxes.

11. Department of Finance, Canada, *Tax Reform 1987, The White Paper* (18 June 1987), p. 34; *Income Tax Reform, Tax Reform* 1987 (18 June 1987), pp. 78-80.

12. Revenue Canada, Interpretation Bulletin IT-218, *Profit from the Sale of Real Estate.*

13. Certain exceptions are "grandfathered" in . So the CCA rate reduction will not affect property you acquire after December 1987 and before 1990 if it's: (1) pursuant to an obligation in writing you enter into before June 18, 1987 for (2) property that was under construction by you or on your behalf on June 18, 1987. Any buildings you acquired before 1988 can continue to be written off at the old rates. As well, you can continue to depreciate post-1987 capital additions to those properties at the old rate to the lesser of $500,000 and 25% of the building's capital cost at December 31, 1987 *or* the date of completion of construction, whichever is later.

192

14. Revenue Canada, Pamphlet 3, *Rental Income.*

15. However, once you dispose of the property—even if you lose money on the disposition—the interest will no longer be deductible. So if, for example, you attempt a high-risk redevelopment but it fails and you sell the property, you could be left with paying off interest charges, but not being able to deduct them.

16. *Loc cit.* Also, see Bulletin IT-434R, *Rental of Real Property by an Individual.*

17. George Fallis, *Housing Programs and Income Distribution in Ontario* (Toronto, 1980).

18. Revenue Canada, IT-120R3, *Principal Residence.*

19. David Baxter, *Urban Land Economics: Speculation in Land,* Discussion paper presented at National Planning Conference, Community Planning Association of Canada, (Regina, Saskatchewan 1974), p 9.

20. Stephen E. Roulac, *Modern Real Estate Investment: An Institutional Approach* (San Francisco, 1976), p. 58.

21. *Ibid.,* p. 8.

22. Samuel Zell, "Modern Sardine Management," *Real Estate Issues* (Spring/ Summer 1986), p. 2.

23. *Study on Tax Considerations in Multi-Family Housing Investment,* U.S. Department of Housing and Urban Development, as cited in Roulac, *op. cit.,* p. 89

24. *Canadian Housing Statistics, 1992,* Canada Mortgage and Housing Corporation, Table 51, p. 55. "Assets and Mortgage Loans of Lending Institutions, 1982-1990."

25. See: Stanley W. Hamilton, David Baxter, Daniel Ulinder, *Foundations of Real Estate Financing: The Mathematical Basis* (Toronto, 1983).

26. All insurer's fees and underwriting standards can change at any time.

27. However, the "balance of sale" does have some advantages for the seller-lender: the seller can demand the cancellation of the sale in the event the debtor defaults in his payments and the seller has the right to foreclose on the property if there's a default on any of the obligations. To the buyer-borrower's benefit, the balance of sale is totally open unless otherwise agreed on.

28. Trading in mortgages is licensed in Nova Scotia, Ontario, Manitoba, Saskatchewan, Alberta, British Columbia and Quebec.

29. *Morehouse et al . v. Income Investments Ltd . et al.* [1966] 1 O.R. 229 (Cty. Ct.).

30. Merle E. Atkins, "Evaluating the Appraisal: Is the Sales Comparison Approach Obsolete?" *National Real Estate Investor* (November, 1986), p. 54.

31. Ontario Real Estate Association, *Principles of Mortgage Financing* (Toronto, 1981), p. xi.

32. On appraisal generally, see: Donald R. Epley, and James H. Boykin, *Basic Income Property Appraisal,* (Don Mills, Ont., 1983); Roulac, *op. cit.,* pp. 341-351; American Institute of Real Estate Appraisers of the National Association of Realtors, *Readings in the Income Approach to Real Property Valuation, Vol. I.* (Chicago, 1977); L.W. Ellwood, *Ellwood Tables for Real Estate Appraising and Financing, Part I Explanatory Text,* (Chicago, 1970).

33. Alan Carson and Robert Dunlop, *Inspecting a House* (Toronto: Stoddart, 1983).

34. Termites aren't a "class" problem . Much of the City of Toronto is termite country, including the trendy areas known as Riverdale, the Beach, Cabbagetown and the West Annex.

35. See: Martin Sclisizzi, "Mortgagee's obligations when selling the property," *Mortgage Remedies 1985,* (Toronto, 1985). *Sterne v. Victoria & Grey Trust Co.* (1984) 49 O.R. (2d) 6 (H.C.I.); *Siskind v. Bank of Nova Scotia* (1984) 46 O.R. (2d) 575. In *Siskind,* the bank as first mortgagee got two appraisals on the property— for $100,000 and $117,500—but sold the property for $70,000, virtually wiping out the second mortgage. A year later the purchaser sold the property for $100,000. In awarding damages to the second mortgagee, the court held that

the bank "fell short of its duty to act in good faith and take reasonable precautions to obtain the true market value of the property."

36. See Richard Arnott, *Rent Control and Options for Decontrol in Ontario* (Toronto, 1981); *Rent Control, A Popular Paradox: Evidence on the Economic Effects of Rent Control* (Vancouver, 1975).

37. Co-operative housing, virtually all of which is federally subsidized, epitomizes the collectivist attitude perfectly when it evicts co-op members who "use too much space." See "Co-op tenant evicted for having too much space," *Toronto Star*, 9 November 1986, C4.

38. For more information, write: your local Ministry of Housing office.

39. Charles Mackay, in his mid-19th Century classic, *Memoirs of Extraordinary Popular Delusions and the Madness of Crowds*, aptly comments on a number of speculative frenzies: Nations, like individuals...have their whims and their peculiarities; their seasons of excitement and recklessness, when they care not what they do. We find that whole communities suddenly fix their minds upon one object, and go mad in its pursuit; that millions of people become simultaneously impressed with one delusion, and run after it, till their attention is caught by some new folly more captivating than the first." Preface to the 1852 Edition, (Toronto, 1980).

40. See Alan Silverstein, *Home-Buying Strategies for Newly-Built Homes* (Toronto: Stoddart, 1987).

41. *Condominium Act,* R.S.O. 1980 c. 84, s. 52(2).

42. Though rent controls limit the revenues the property owner can receive, the revenue potential is still there. Only it's appropriated by tenants who assign their leases in exchange for the "price" of their old carpeting, curtains and the like.

43. S.W. Hamilton, ed., *Condominiums: A decade of experience in B.C.* (Vancouver, 1978), p. 18

44. Toronto Real Estate Board, *House Price Trends. Op. cit.*

45. According to Tridel Corp. in "Condo fever is sweeping Metro Toronto," *Toronto Star* advertising feature, 22 October 1986, B9.

46. Terminology, and the precise meaning of the *same* terms, differs across the country.

47. Condominium ownership has also been successfully applied to small industrial units, where it has had some appeal to investors but is more suited to owner occupiers. As well, medical condominiums have proven popular for medical professionals. And there has been a limited application of the condominium form to office, retail and hotel space.

48. Between 1979 and 1984 in Metro Toronto, for instance, the average apartment resale price rose 62% vs. 44.46% for all residential sales and 27.6% for townhouse resales. The soaring price of apartments though, was due to the sea of luxury units introduced in the early '80s, which was a tremendous change from the earlier idea of condominiums as "affordable" housing. More recently, condominium resale average prices have been closely tracking residential properties generally. See: Toronto Real Estate Board, *House Price Trends, Op. cit.*

49. Terminology and requirements differ from province to province. In Saskatchewan, for instance, regulations and by-laws must be in a standard form. In some, by-laws aren't required or refer not to living rules but to the project's basic organization. In Ontario, each developer can write his own documents, none of which are vetted by any authority whatsoever.

50. *The Condominium Property Act*, s. 26(1).

51. *Strata Titles Act*, S.B.C., 1966, ch. 46, s. 33.

194

52.   Ontario requires the developer to pay the buyer interest during the interim occupancy period.

53.   As long as the deposit is not so large as to be a penalty or unconscionable, and is not merely intended to be part payment, the seller can retain the deposit. The leading case on this point, *Howe v. Smith* (1884), 27 Ch.D. 89 (C.A.), says that " . . . in the event of the contract being performed, [the deposit] shall be brought into account, but if the contract is not performed by the payer, it shall remain the property of the payee. It is not merely a part payment, but is also then an earnest to bind the bargain so entered into and creates by the fear of its forfeiture a motive in the payee to perform the rest of the contract." See, also: *Lejbak v. Tucker* (1982), 16 Sask. R. 409 (Q.B.) wherein the Court notes that the decision in *Howe* "has been consistently approved by the Canadian courts."

54.   Civil Code, 1659.7.

55.   *H. W. Liebig and Company Ltd. v. Leading Investments Ltd.* [1986] S.C.R. 70.

56.   For a full explanation of daily interest rate calculation and its unacceptable alternatives, see: Daniel Ulinder, "Canadian Lending Practices: A Review and Commentary on the Basis of Mortgage Interest and Balance Determination," *Education Quarterly*, (Spring 1984), pp. 12-20.

57.   However, every regulating province has its own variations, some written and some by the interpretation of the responsible administrators.

    If you live in Saskatchewan, for instance, you can lend money on mortgages without regulation as long as you don't lend on more than five mortgages in a calendar year. In Ontario, the Registrar says that if you buy and hold a mortgage to maturity, you're not a broker. Also, in Ontario, all real estate brokers are automatically mortgage brokers.

    Lawyers are usually specifically exempt from regulation. And even in Ontario, where they aren't, they regularly ignore the *Mortgage Brokers Act*, contending as a group that they are not covered by it. Despite his annoyance, Ontario's Registrar hasn't taken action. He says that borrowers and lenders are perhaps better protected by access to Law Society funds in case the lawyer acts improperly than by provincial registration.

    Certainly, registration didn't prevent the multi-million dollar losses inflicted on investors in the failures of Re-Mor/Astre Trust and Argosy Financial in Ontario and the voluntary liquidation of Dial Mortgage in Alberta.

58.   The discount process is the same as when a vendor sells a VTB mortgage at the time of the sale.

59.   "Ex-lawyer admits stealing $2 million." *Toronto Star*, 15 April 1984. A few years later, another Ontario lawyer upped the ante, and was eventually disbarred for misappropriating and misapplying approximately $10 million of client money. He claimed to be registering first mortgages but none were actually first mortgages.,

60.   These and other U.S. MBS can be purchased through U.S. investment dealers. Besides buying the securities directly, you can participate in the U.S. market through MBS mutual funds, unit trusts and collateralized mortgage obligations (bonds backed by mortgage securities and directly by mortgages themselves).

61.   For fuller explanation of the factors affecting yield, see Merrill Lynch Canada Inc. publications: *Merrill Lynch Canada Inc. Explains NHA Mortgage-backed Securities* and *Pricing Considerations for Mortgage-backed Securities*. (1986).

62.   Royal Trust figures.

63.   Each province has its own regulations on these matters. For specifics in your area, contact your provincial securities commission. Also see, *CCH Securities Law Reporter*, available in most major libraries.

64. "Consortium boss convicted in absentia." *Toronto Star*, 5 June 1991 p. D-3.

65. Typically, rent control tribunals aren't burdened with following formal rules of evidence or procedural safeguards governing other administrative tribunals.

66. However, in some circumstances, tenants are empowered to withhold rents in excess of permitted increases. See: "An Act to provide for the Regulation of Rents charged for Rental Units in Residential Complexes," S.O. 1986, c. 63, s. 73.

67. *Sterne v. Victoria & Grey Trust Co., Supra*, endnote 35.

68. R.S.M. 1970, c. R20, s.19 (10).

69. *Ella v. Perlman*, [1961] O.W.N. 200 (S.C.).

70. R.S.M. 1970 c. R20, s.19 (2),(3).

71. R.S.N.B. 1973, c. R-l (s.23) (2) (c).

72. *D'Altri v. Chilcott* [1975], 55 D.L.R. (3d) 30 (Ont. S.C.).

73. *Palinko v. Bower* [1976] 4 WWR 118 (Alta. C.A.); *Kramer v. Cooper*, [1975]. 2W. W.R. I (B.C.S.C.).

74. D.J. Donahue and P.D. Quinn, *Real Estate Practice in Ontario, 3rd ed.* (Toronto, 1982), p. 88 (emphasis added).